101 TIPS FOR TEACHING

practical advice for everyone who imparts truth

MARK RASMUSSEN

First published in 2007 by Striving Together Publications, a
ministry of Lancaster Baptist Church, Lancaster, CA 93535.
Striving Together Publications is committed to providing tried,
trusted, and proven books that will further equip local churches
to carry out the Great Commission. Your comments and
suggestions are valued.

Striving Together Publications
4020 E. Lancaster Blvd.
Lancaster, CA 93535
800.201.7748

Cover design by Andrew Jones
Layout by Craig Parker
Edited by Danielle Mordh
Special thanks to our proofreaders.

ISBN 978-1-59894-031-2

Printed in the United States of America

CONTENTS

Part 2—Things We Should Do

DEDICATION

Dedicated to parents, pastors, and teachers who have a passion to see the mind of Christ developed in those God has entrusted to their watch care.

INTRODUCTION

The Apostle Paul, under the influence of the Holy Spirit, said, "I am Debtor." Today, reflecting on twenty-nine years in Christian education as a teacher and seventeen years as a student, I echo his words.

I am debtor to godly parents, who after viewing one year of public education in my life, paid the personal and ministerial price to start a Christian school in large part to protect their own children from secular humanism. I am a debtor for their example of what a Christian marriage should be like and for a total dedication in their lives to put the work of Christ above all else.

I am debtor to a great elementary teacher, Jeannie Prehmus, who loved me and used creative methods to give me a heart to read. Her passion for the transference of knowledge is still palpable after the passing of almost four decades. The hundreds who were honored to be under her tutelage have been unanimous in their thanks and praise.

I am debtor to a high school teacher named Dave Fizz who modeled consistency in his love for his Lord, his Pastor, and his students. I am thankful for his example in a daily walk with the Lord. In many ways Brother Fizz was the ultimate example of a trustworthy and loyal team member who had a love for his students and a heart to lighten his Pastor's burdens.

I am debtor to a great college teacher, Dr. Wendell Evans. I will always be thankful that he would carve time from a hectic schedule to discuss books and ideas with an impressionable college student. I will always be indebted for his entrusting me with the opportunity to teach on the college level as a very young man and coaching and cajoling me to strive for excellence.

I am debtor to Pastor Paul Chappell for showing me through both his life and teaching definitive servant leadership. I also thank Pastor Chappell and Brother Jerry Ferrso for their challenge in the area of personal soulwinning. They have both taught me by their lives as well as their words.

I am a debtor to co-laborers in the pulpit and classroom who challenge me with their faithfulness, sacrifice, and friendship over the decades. An exemplary influence over the last decade has been Dr. John Goetsch. His example of discipline, dedication, and work ethic has been a continual challenge.

I am debtor to myriad friends and co-laborers who have shared these truths thus impacting my life. Some were caught by watching your example, others were taught.

I am debtor to my wife. For over twenty-five years, she has taught me so much about the Christian life. Her patience, kindness, gentleness, and meekness have helped and encouraged me more then she will ever know.

Finally, and above all, my greatest debt is to my Lord who loved me and gave Himself for me. He truly is the Master Teacher. It is my prayer that all who read this book will come to know Him and then strive to be like Him.

Part 1

Things We Should Know

1

TIP #1

It's All in Your Attitude

"A wrathful man stirreth up strife: but he that is slow to anger appeaseth strife."—PROVERBS 15:18

"A soft answer turneth away wrath: but grievous words stir up anger."—PROVERBS 15:1

The study of great coaches and leaders will sometimes reveal men of immense acidic and acerbic personalities (men such as Bobby Knight, Vince Lombardi, and Richard Nixon). I have always thought, however, that I would like my coach or my mentor to be one who is kind and positive.

Once, while sitting in the den of John Wooden, the great basketball coach of UCLA, I heard someone ask him the question, "What is the most important trait for a leader?" His answer was quite surprising. He said, "He must be a good listener." Having a kind, listening spirit allows one to mentor and instruct far more thoroughly than if one was to be overly reactive, caustic, or cruel.

In Proverbs, the greatest book of wisdom ever written, Solomon wrote, "*The sweetness of the lips increaseth learning.*" The instructor needs to remember that the tongue is a little member that can cause a great fire or bring vast encouragement. In the words of that great philosopher Mary Poppins, "A spoonful of sugar helps the medicine go down." We need to be experts at looking for and commending the good.

Oftentimes, an instructor can spot a malefactor committing the most minor of grievances at a distance of 400 yards. He will draw down on him like a bow hunter ready for the instantaneous kill on the first day of deer season. Conversely, if the instructor would have the same amount of attention directed toward those who are doing right, attitudes would undoubtedly be affected. In short, the Golden Rule will help us as we strive to remember to treat others the way we would like to be treated.

2

TIP #2

Try is the Father of Triumph

"For a just man falleth seven times, and riseth up again: but the wicked shall fall into mischief."—Proverbs 24:16

It has often been said, "The only place where success comes before work is in the dictionary." God's Word says in Ecclesiastes 9:10, "*Whatsoever thy hand findeth to do, do it with thy might....*" Teddy Roosevelt once said, "It is better to have tried and failed than never to have tried at all."

Often, tasks are not accomplished because goals have not been set and little has been expected. The instructor needs to create expectations that will take effort to accomplish. One of his priority goals should be to get the student to make an attempt at new and difficult things. "I can't," seems to have become the rally cry for today's society. Oftentimes, "I can't" really means, "I won't." But in reality, people will not know if they can or can't do something unless they first put forth an effort to accomplish the appointed task.

As a seventh grade boy, my father wanted me to learn how to water-ski. I stated that I did not like water-skiing and that I did not want to go. I wanted to stay at the camp and play basketball and ping-pong. These were my comfort zones. These were things I already knew how to do. I had tried water-skiing only once or twice in my life, and I had not succeeded at it.

My father told me I did not have to stay at the lake, but every day I had to try at least three times. By the second day, I learned how to get on top of the water and ride the skis. Not long after, I learned how to drop a ski, and how to get up on a single ski. Water-skiing eventually became one of the great joys of my teenage years. I will ever be thankful my father forced me to leave my comfort zone.

Whether at soulwinning, being friendly, learning to appreciate books, or excelling at a certain skill, let's encourage people to obey God's Word, which commands us to do things with all of our might. This truly is an excellent definition of trying.

3

TIP #3

Inspiration Often Precedes Education

"And by knowledge shall the chambers be filled with all precious and pleasant riches."—Proverbs 24:4

"Who is as the wise man? and who knoweth the interpretation of a thing? a man's wisdom maketh his face to shine, and the boldness of his face shall be changed."—Ecclesiastes 8:1

For the engine of learning to begin to turn, there must be a fire built in the furnace of inspiration. It is this furnace that fuels, drives, and motivates the student to gain or acquire knowledge and truth.

Part of the inspirational process involves the student's understanding why something is important. The instructor cannot fail to remember that people tend to give time to that which they feel is important. We carve out expenditures of energy on that which we feel is important. We spend our money on that which we think is important. Therefore, we need to inspire the student to grasp the importance of the subject, principle, or truth being taught.

The preaching of the Word of God is the easiest venue through which inspiration may occur. Biblical principles are principles that are eternal. They procure life change. It is up to the instructor to allow these truths to captivate, change, and redirect the heart of the student.

It also must be clearly stated that if the student does not think these principles are important to the teacher, he certainly will not place value on them. This is where personal testimonies of what these truths have meant or done in our lives will help to show value to the listener.

It is more difficult to inspire students in secular subjects, but showing the practicality of a certain subject will inspire them to learn the subject at hand. In the field of history, there are facts considered general knowledge. In the field of business, there are issues of budgeting, investing, and comprehension of what compounded interest can do either for or against a person. In the area of science, explanations can be given to show a person the hand of God and the order which He has created the world. Seek to inspire your students to learn in every aspect of their education.

4

TIP #4

Maximum Involvement Equals Maximum Learning

"The heart of him that hath understanding seeketh knowledge: but the mouth of fools feedeth on foolishness."
—Proverbs 15:14

Due to the incredible influence of television and videos, the young people in today's society tend to be extraordinarily passive. This non-interaction, fostered predominantly by television, not only involves a lack of physical activity, but a lack of thinking as well. When reading books (rather than watching television and other media) was at the core of the educational process, creativity, and imagination were fostered.

Today's instructor must realize that the student has been accustomed to being merely a passive receptor. Involving him in the learning process will take the student out of the customary comfort zone and push him toward greater heights of learning.

Drawing the student out of the comfort zone ought to be the primary goal of every instructor. The student must not be allowed simply *to watch.* He must be *involved* in the learning process.

One of the best ways to involve students is to ask them to explain the principle that has just been taught. Learning to critique, evaluate, and articulate helps the student to formulate and analyze in a way that will enable him to understand and remember.

Most instructors have as a goal for their students that they will retain information. One must understand that retention is a byproduct and an aftereffect of concentration. Concentration will not occur, however, if the students are not involved in the educational process. When teaching a Bible story, for instance, it is very effective for students to imagine themselves in the scene. Playacting or drama allows the student to visualize a truth being taught.

The more the student can be involved with the instructor and the process, the greater the learning and ultimate retention will be.

5

TIP #5

Practice Makes Permanent

"Give instruction to a wise man, and he will be yet wiser: teach a just man, and he will increase in learning."
—Proverbs 9:9

Whether it was the learning of the Palmer Method or the repetitive quotations of the times tables, there is not an adult today who does not remember the repetition and practice that were used to make a certain skill a part of one's life.

Whether involved in the secular or sacred realm, one of the problems with today's educational method is the lack of repetition on certain core principles, knowledge skills, or beliefs. While it is true that some things are easily mastered, other things only become a part of our nature and can be done without having to stop, think, and prepare because we have practiced them so many times.

It is easy to remember the practice that was involved in first learning how to ride a bicycle without training wheels. With each additional practice run, the skill level increased until finally it became second nature. Possibly it was learning to write with a certain style, or maybe it was learning to write one's name until an individuality and a uniqueness became ownership.

Character skills—whether it is the seating of a young lady, saying "Yes, ma'am" or "No, ma'am" or "Yes, sir" or "No, sir"—will all ultimately become habitual if they are practiced enough.

Not long ago a national publication told of a church leader, well into his eighties, who had to walk using a walker. They discussed the laborious effort that took place upon his exiting a limousine, which was carrying him and his wife. It told how he carefully made his way around the car to open the door for his wife of over sixty years. Someone commented on this to the church leader and he stated, "I learned to do that a long time ago."

The instructor needs to realize that the things he is making the student practice and learn are those things that can ultimately become part of what makes the student's character.

6

TIP #6

Reading is to the Mind What Exercise is to the Body

"Study to shew thyself approved unto God, a workman that needeth not to be ashamed, rightly dividing the word of truth."—2 Timothy 2:15

Muscles left to themselves will inevitably atrophy. Anyone who has ever had a broken limb encased in a plaster cast will see the unmistakable results of atrophy after the cast is removed. It is not that anything bad has happened to the muscle, but rather, nothing happened to the muscle during that time.

In much the same way, the mind can atrophy if it is not used. *Reader's Digest* has done a series of articles on the importance of senior citizens' exercising their minds. Items such as crossword puzzles, games, and books on a variety of subjects have seemed to help keep the mind sharp.

The instructor must understand that students must be provided with good information to read in order to keep their minds sharp. This starts with the biblical premise that we are to think about things that are true, just, lovely, and of good report (Philippians 4:8), and would be polar opposite to most of the popular fiction that is being consumed by many Christian teenagers today.

Reading provides help in the areas of spelling, concentration, and comprehension skills. More importantly, reading helps to reveal areas in which students can learn and be helped. Determine to encourage the exercising of the mind through reading.

7

TIP #7

The Biggest Room in a Life is the Room for Improvement

"I press toward the mark for the prize of the high calling of God in Christ Jesus."—Philippians 3:14

"The status quo," "the norm," "the way we are,"—these phrases are replete with the spirit of defeatism. The student must understand that there is always room for growth and improvement.

God's Word commands us to grow *"in the nurture and admonition of the Lord"* (Ephesians 6:4). In 1 Peter 2:2 the Bible says that we are to grow from spiritual babes on a diet of milk, to spiritual adults on a diet of meat. The Apostle Paul, at the end of his ministry, was not content to rest and reflect while sitting in a prison cell. He asked his faithful follower Timothy to bring him the books and especially the parchments.

Even while his earthly ministry was dwindled to its few final days, this giant of the New Testament wanted to continue to grow, to learn, and to sharpen himself.

Those who truly understand the heart of the Lord and the mind of Christ realize the necessity for continued growth and learning. This growth goes beyond the boundaries of academia into skills and character qualities as well.

My own father, who in his seventies was still studying his Greek on a daily basis, memorizing verses, and reviewing the thousands of verses he had previously committed to memory, challenged me. I asked him why he continued to study Greek at such an advanced age. He said, "God tells us to occupy until He comes."

Every instructor, whether parent or teacher, must realize that *potential* is a word that, while sometimes overused, is also frequently never realized.

8

TIP #8

Choose What is Right over What is Easy

"I beseech you therefore, brethren, by the mercies of God, that ye present your bodies a living sacrifice, holy, acceptable unto God, which is your reasonable service."—ROMANS 12:1

"Yea doubtless, and I count all things but loss for the excellency of the knowledge of Christ Jesus my Lord: for whom I have suffered the loss of all things, and do count them but dung, that I may win Christ,"—PHILIPPIANS 3:8

Seldom are worthwhile accomplishments achieved in life without a conscientious effort being put forth. There is a price to pay when one decides to be consistent in exercise in either the spiritual or physical realm. There is a price to pay to graduate from high school. There is a price to pay to graduate from college. There is a price to pay to memorize Scripture and to be truly devoted to reading and studying. There is a price to pay to have a good marriage. There is a price to pay when one chooses to rear children over letting them rear themselves. There is a price to pay when one truly decides to be soul-conscious and to pray more. There is a price to pay when one truly wants to learn God's Word. There is a price to pay when one decides to learn and be edified by every message that is heard.

There are prices to pay in the accomplishment of any worthy goal. It is the job of the instructor to help the learner understand that nothing good will ever come without a price. Choosing what is right over that which is easy is always the difficult choice. It runs contrary to human nature. However, when people begin to see the results of choosing that which is right over that which is easy, there can truly be a change in one's life direction.

9

TIP #9

MANDATORY ENTHUSIASM

"Whatsoever is commanded by the God of heaven, let it be diligently done for the house of the God of heaven...."
—EZRA 7:23

There are many possessions or characteristics a teacher may not have and still be successful. He may not have new clothes, an up-to-date car, or what the world calls "physical attractiveness." Nevertheless, one needed quality is enthusiasm about the subject at hand.

It can be guaranteed that the student will never be more interested in the subject than the instructor. You may be thinking to yourself, "It is hard for me to get excited about this subject." You may think your enthusiasm must be feigned, but that is not the answer. The student will know whether or not you really care about the topic you are discussing.

If God allows us the privilege of teaching a particular subject or a particular age group, we need to be excited about the opportunity God has given us. Although it may not have been our own personal choice, we need to realize that others could be jealous of the opportunity that is ours, and we must thank God for every opportunity He gives us.

We must also realize that it is important to find a part of the subject about which we can be enthusiastic. I heard it said many years ago, "If we would not be fired with enthusiasm, we would be *fired* with enthusiasm!"

I believe it is imperative to understand that, as teachers, our genuine interest, love, and enthusiasm for the topic at hand is the spark that kindles the fire of learning.

10

TIP #10

Ordinary People Must Have Extraordinary Dedication

"And of some have compassion, making a difference:"
—JUDE 1:22

Geniuses are few and far between. The extraordinary parent or teacher who does every action with such excitement and creativity that their children seem to always respond with great results, is truly one-in-a-million!

While it is always interesting to read the stories of teachers who have received awards (such as the Teacher-of-the-Year Award), it must be understood that the majority of us do not have genius IQs or Einstein and Edison-level creativity! What we do have is an opportunity to dedicate ourselves to do life-changing work as emissaries of the Lord Jesus Christ.

If we will teach in ways that will touch lives forever, then we must be willing to go the extra mile. We must be willing to pay the price that is necessary to achieve excellence. Parents must be willing to spend the time interacting with their children—talking and training.

Dedication involves planning, follow-through, and attitude. All of these must be combined to achieve extraordinary results. We must realize that we can do this and all things through Christ. We can, with God's help, impact a life that will make a difference for the cause of Christ, both now and for eternity.

11

TIP #11

God Does not Want Anything Other than Our Everything

"Neither yield ye your members as instruments of unrighteousness unto sin: but yield yourselves unto God, as those that are alive from the dead, and your members as instruments of righteousness unto God."—Romans 6:13

"And this they did, not as we hoped, but first gave their own selves to the Lord, and unto us by the will of God."
—2 Corinthians 8:5

The songwriter penned the words, "All to Jesus I surrender, all to Him I freely give." These words are far easier to sing than they are to live! God has created us for the purpose of serving Him, and He deserves every aspect of our lives, hearts, and talents.

Children today need to be taught the bondservant principle. They must realize they have been *"bought with a price"* (1 Corinthians 6:20), and they are truly not their own (1 Corinthians 6:19).

D.L. Moody said, "The world has yet to see what God can do with one man who is totally yielded to Him." Moody went on to say that by God's grace he would be that man. This man, with limited education, shook two continents for the cause of the Lord Jesus Christ, because he was willing to give his all.

Charles Cowman, the great missionary to Asia in the early twentieth century, desired to give his all. David Brainerd, William Carey, and many others desired to give their all. One look in the "Hall of Faith" (Hebrews 11) reveals men who were willing to give their all. Are you willing to give God your all? Are your students surrendered to the Lord?

Instructors must challenge their pupils to be living sacrifices willing to give God everything.

12

TIP #12

For the Believer, All Ground is Holy Ground

"Whether therefore ye eat, or drink, or whatsoever ye do, do all to the glory of God."—1 Corinthians 10:31

It has been said that for the Christian, there is no difference between the secular and the sacred. All aspects of our lives should be characterized by holiness and sanctification. I believe we must live lives that are set apart for the cause of the Lord Jesus Christ.

The student must also understand that true Christianity is to be lived every moment of every day. He should be daily dedicated to preparing for the return of the Master. When the student understands that all ground is holy ground, he responds to correction based on the principles of the Word of God. Principles such as, "*Obey them that have the rule over you…for they watch for your souls…*" (Hebrews 13:17). He plays on the playground with attitudes and actions that are dictated by the Word of God, which says, "*And be ye kind one to another, tenderhearted, forgiving one another, even as God for Christ's sake hath forgiven you*" (Ephesians 4:32). The principles and illustrations are almost infinite in number. When the student truly understands this concept, he will know that, regardless of the situation, he is on holy ground.

Finally, the instructor must remember that even in the midst of stress or pressure, he is also standing on holy ground and must strive to do all his work for the glory of God.

13

TIP #13

Ignoring Discipline is Inviting Disaster

"He that spareth his rod hateth his son: but he that loveth him chasteneth him betimes."—Proverbs 13:24

Discipline is a subject that is often neglected because it is difficult to discuss and often creates an uncomfortable response. If discipline is ignored, however, tragedy will ultimately ensue. This tragedy may not be noticeable in the short-term, but it will wreak havoc and long-term consequences for the student.

Discipline must involve a plan which includes both guidelines and consequences. The student must clearly know what is required and prohibited, and understand that if the rules are broken, there will be earned consequences. (Consequences are somewhat easier to understand than punishment.)

The critical link of discipline is that while sometimes there are clearly stated rules and consequences, often, the follow-through does not take place. It will not take the student long to understand whether or not the instructor means what he says.

In addition to a lack of follow-through, another great enemy of consistent discipline is over-familiarity. This is a teacher who wants to be a "buddy" instead of an instructor. This invariably reaps failure because the student does not expect a relationship with a friend to be primarily a teaching and learning relationship.

Lack of consistent discipline on the part of the instructor will often create tension in the students and disaster in the classroom. Persistent follow-through coupled with a right spirit will ensure effective discipline and academic accomplishment in the school and home.

14

TIP #14

Children Are a Precious Treasure

"But the Lord *said unto Samuel, Look not on his countenance, or on the height of his stature; because I have refused him: for the* Lord *seeth not as man seeth; for man looketh on the outward appearance, but the* Lord *looketh on the heart."*
—1 Samuel 16:7

As our girls were entering their teen years, my wife prayed one night, "Lord, please help us as we rear these girls. We have never done this before." I have referred to that simple statement often for well over a decade. Whether it be our students, children, or others' children, we have only one attempt to get it right!

I once heard someone say, "I don't think most teachers realize how much impact they have." As teachers, we should never underestimate the value of a life and the impact one life can make. Amazingly, the lives that make the most impact often initially go unnoticed by everyone else. Many times as I have looked at my classes, I have thought, "I wonder if there is a David in here, the brother who is not thought to be a king, and yet the one who would ultimately be the man after God's own heart."

Our prayer should be for God to help us realize our incredible responsibility and opportunity each time we impart truth to those precious treasures God entrusts to us.

15

TIP #15

TEACHING EQUALS TRAINING

"But none of these things move me, neither count I my life dear unto myself, so that I might finish my course with joy, and the ministry, which I have received of the Lord Jesus, to testify the gospel of the grace of God."—ACTS 20:24

"Remembering without ceasing your work of faith, and labour of love, and patience of hope in our Lord Jesus Christ, in the sight of God and our Father;"—1 THESSALONIANS 1:3

Training involves a multiplicity of effects. Teaching could be defined as educating, instructing, enlightening, and preparing. It involves leading, rearing, guiding, and shaping. It could also mean encouraging, infusing, and nurturing. But, above all, teaching is training.

God's Word says, "*Train up a child in the way he should go: and when he is old, he will not depart from it*" (Proverbs 22:6). Training involves a process whereby new skills are learned and a character change is effected.

Teaching is more than just discussing a subject in which the instructor is an expert. It involves training the student to also become an expert in that subject. We teach someone how to ride a bike so he can ride by himself. We teach someone correct grammar so he can speak correctly. We teach someone how to have devotions so he can have a personal devotional walk. We teach someone how to lead a soul to Christ so he can win the lost to Christ.

One of the most efficient ways to ensure that our teaching equals the student's training is by allowing them to teach someone else. This will place into practice that which he has been taught.

It must never be forgotten that Jesus spent three years teaching and training His disciples before sending them out to literally turn their world upside down for the cause of Christ.

May His example motivate us to train the children in our care before sending them forth to be used of God to accomplish great works for His glory.

16

TIP #16

A Good Plan Done is Better than a Great Plan Dreamed

"The desire accomplished is sweet to the soul: but it is abomination to fools to depart from evil."—PROVERBS 13:19

"O love the LORD, all ye his saints: for the LORD preserveth the faithful, and plentifully rewardeth the proud doer." —PSALM 31:23

"But be ye doers of the word, and not hearers only, deceiving your own selves."—JAMES 1:22

Years ago, my first boss in Christian work told me about a man who was full of great dreams. He said, "This gentleman has more ideas than we can put into place if we worked at it for one hundred years. It would be good if he had just a few ideas that could actually be implemented."

It is wise to encourage young people to have goals. Yet teaching them to put action to their plans is just as vital. Oftentimes, grandiose dreams of projects, inventions, and visions of grandeur are never begun.

Many folks are afraid to start because they are afraid to fail. It is better to have tried and failed than to have never tried at all. It is a wonderful thing to create a list of things one wants to accomplish in a semester, a year, or even a lifetime, yet the student must be encouraged to go beyond the list-making to actively pursuing the accomplishment. People are not remembered for their ideas or intentions; they are remembered by how they start and how they finish. It is imperative that they learn how to finish a job.

A school teacher once said, "A hundred years from now it will not matter what my bank account was, the sort of house I lived in, or the kind of car I drove...but the world may be different because I was important in the life of a child." May we be teachers who make a difference because we encourage not only great dreams, but the execution and completion of good plans.

17

TIP #17

No Time Like the Present, No Present Like Your Time

"Boast not thyself of to morrow; for thou knowest not what a day may bring forth."—Proverbs 27:1

Many are familiar with the Ron Hamilton song for children that includes the phrase, "Do it now, don't delay. Don't put it off 'til another day." The instructor's time to teach, train, and impact students' lives is today! We truly know not what the morrow will bring. We have no guarantee that we will ever have a learning or teaching opportunity again.

"Nothing is a waste of time if you use the experience wisely."

The Latin phrase *carpe diem* means, "Seize the day." This phrase could be something the Christian instructor feels with far more intensity than someone from the secular world. It is the Christian instructor who understands that we are to work for the night is coming. We must have a keen understanding that our lives truly are like a vapor.

Because of this urgency, we need to realize the greatest thing we can give to the student is our time. The most casual or even caustic student will appreciate the gift of the instructor's time.

Pastor Chappell often says, "People do not care how much you know until they know how much you care." Are you communicating your care through the giving of your time? The investment truly is a worthy one.

18

TIP #18

Dissatisfaction with the Status Quo

"That he may incline our hearts unto him, to walk in all his ways, and to keep his commandments, and his statutes, and his judgments, which he commanded our fathers."
—1 Kings 8:58

Contentment is a very important facet of the Christian life that needs to be stressed. Yet, a healthy dissatisfaction with the status quo can bring about growth. It has been said that a rut is nothing more than a grave with the ends knocked out. It is imperative, then, for the instructor to get his class out of a rut and to encourage growth in the lives of his students!

It does take effort to get students moving in the right direction, yet this effort is often predicated simply with the initial challenge given by a mentor. We must teach and motivate our students to be dissatisfied with the "average" and to passionately strive for that which is pleasing to Christ.

In addition to challenging the next generation to grow, it is essential that young people see a desire for improvement, growth, and godly attainment in their parents and schoolteachers. As mentors, if we will model this healthy dissatisfaction with the status quo, it will then become much easier to help students in needed areas.

While it is important to emphasize growth in the life and mind of the student, it is even more important to emphasize the place of God in his life. If God is the goal, growth will occur.

Yes, it is important to be content, but do not be satisfied with giving anything less than your best to the Lord. Are you truly accomplishing tasks with all your might (Ecclesiastes 9:10)? Are you truly working in a way that would bring glory to God (1 Corinthians 10:31)? If not, then ask God for that healthy dissatisfaction and strive to exceed the status quo for the Saviour.

19

TIP #19

The Inattentive Mind Neither Sees nor Hears

"Casting down imaginations, and every high thing that exalteth itself against the knowledge of God, and bringing into captivity every thought to the obedience of Christ;" —2 Corinthians 10:5

"Wherefore, my beloved brethren, let every man be swift to hear, slow to speak, slow to wrath:"—James 1:19

Attention must be guarded in order for learning to take place. In many ways, the mind is like a blank canvass waiting for the instructor to paint a panorama of truth upon it. It must be understood that this canvass is not accessible if the door to the mind has not been opened. This door of attention is not always readily moved, however, and sometimes different implements must be used in order to gain access to the mind of the student. Here, the instructor needs to make use of the tools that are in his hand to communicate truth.

An educational parable compared the inattentive student to a deaf and blind man—the inattentive mind neither sees nor hears. It would obviously be a difficult task to communicate truth to such a person. It is imperative, then, for the teacher to make it the highest priority to secure the total concentration of the student. He must constantly think and plan for ways to rein in attention.

Attention could be visualized as a wild horse that, until broken and controlled, is of little productive use. While watching a wild horse run across a verdant field is a beautiful sight, in reality, the horse is of little real usefulness. Likewise, the mind is of no substantial use if it is not controlled and brought into focus. The mind must be reined in and brought to attention regarding the issue at hand.

God's Word states that every thought is to be brought into subjection. The instructor must help students bring thoughts into subjection and into the arena of the subject matter being communicated.

20

TIP #20

Increased Predictability Lowers Impact

"A merry heart doeth good like a medicine: but a broken spirit drieth the bones."—Proverbs 17:22

"To every thing there is a season, and a time to every purpose under the heaven:"—Ecclesiastes 3:1

Variety is the spice of life! Therefore, instructors must use a multiplicity of methods and approaches to achieve maximum impact in the lives of their students.

Phrases such as: "Same old stuff," "Always the same," "Never anything new," and "Usually boring," are often statements made by students to describe the predictable instructor who never varies in his methods or materials. This instructor greatly limits the potential growth and gain of the students if he refuses to change his teaching styles.

We can vary our teaching in many ways: using humor, walking around the classroom, reversing the usual order of schedule, or incorporating visual aids. These actions must be done in order to both gain and keep the students' attention.

Preparation is the key to impacting the mind of the students. In the arena of sports, the athlete knows he has power that comes from the transfer of energy from the back leg to the front leg. He will only reach maximum impact when the torso is involved. This is true in throwing a ball, swinging a bat, or throwing a punch.

In order for us as instructors to have maximum impact, we must ensure that preparation has preceded the teaching moment. Our power to impact comes from prayer and preparation. If we are not prepared, the students will lose respect and interest.

Do you want to increase your impact as a teacher? Then lower your predictability! Become passionate about effectively teaching through a variety of methods.

21

TIP #21
Practice Increases Performance

"Let your heart therefore be perfect with the Lord *our God, to walk in his statutes, and to keep his commandments, as at this day."*—1 Kings 8:61

"For Ezra had prepared his heart to seek the law of the Lord, *and to do it, and to teach in Israel statutes and judgments."*—Ezra 7:10

The common adage is that "practice makes perfect." I am afraid that most teachers would beg to differ with that phrase! Not all practice leads to perfection! (In all probability, it is very unlikely for something to be done perfectly or exactly right.) However, practice *does* usually lead to improved performance and a well-done job, so it is an extremely important discipline to be taught.

Repetition creates both the proper mindset and the proper memory of how to carry out certain actions when an actual event occurs. This principle is necessary in the realm of teaching young people to make right choices. If they are confronted with problems and practice making the right choices, they will build a subconscious, Christ-honoring response.

It is very unlikely for the student to practice without a great deal of encouragement. Therefore, if practice is to take place, it must be encouraged, directed, and often even mandated by the instructor. Parents and teachers of those in elementary school are cognizant of the numerous reminders it takes to instill the habitual response of "Yes, sir," or "No, sir," and "Yes, ma'am," or "No, ma'am." Whether in Scripture reading, prayer time, or soulwinning, the young person must be encouraged and directed to practice these actions.

Despite opposition to the contrary, the instructor will realize that time spent in practice will always reap great dividends in the performance.

22

TIP #22

Can't Usually Means *Won't*

"Therefore to him that knoweth to do good, and doeth it not, to him it is sin."—James 4:17

After a young child learns his first negative word, "No!" one of the next words to enter his vocabulary is the word, "*can't*." It is important for the instructor to understand and illustrate to the student that "*can't*" frequently means "*won't*."

The Bible clearly states, "*I can do all things through Christ which strengtheneth me*" (Philippians 4:13). Especially in areas of biblical obedience (such as giving, witnessing, discipling, or holy living), we must explain and illustrate that while we cannot do these actions in and of ourselves, we *can* do them through Christ! God's grace is sufficient (2 Corinthians 12:9), and we need Him.

Another effective way to remove this negative response from the student is to demonstrate how he is capable of accomplishing what was thought to be impossible, or at least exceedingly difficult. Help the student to see areas in which he has succeeded through Christ's strength.

Personal illustrations may also be valuable in helping a student feel that he is accepted and helping him to understand that he is not alone when facing a difficulty or dilemma. The Bible illustrates this personal identification in Scripture when it states that Jesus Christ "*...was in all points tempted like as we are, yet without sin*" (Hebrews 4:15).

If we allow our students to say that they cannot do that which has been commanded by God, we are enabling them to give place to the devil, and we must not allow the defeated one to have victory in our lives! May we teach our students that if they know to do good and refuse to do it—it is sin! May we encourage them that they truly *can* do *all* things through Christ who strengthens them!

23

TIP #23

Actions Speak Louder Than Words

"Let no man despise thy youth; but be thou an example of the believers, in word, in conversation, in charity, in spirit, in faith, in purity."—1 Timothy 4:12

Almost three decades ago in a Bible college leadership class, I was reminded of this phrase, "Our walk talks louder than our talk talks." What a great truth summarized in a few words! It is of utmost importance for any parent or teacher to realize that one's life carries an incredible weight in the educational process.

As mentors, the greatest gift we can give is our example. This should lead each of us to ask questions of ourselves regarding what we are modeling. When was the last time we were seen praying at the altar? When was the last time we were seen walking a convert down the aisle? When was the last time we were seen spontaneously and naturally giving a tract or witnessing? When was the last time we were seen doing a random act of kindness? These examples often have a far greater, long-term result than a carefully prepared lecture.

Instructors, remember that the students are watching to see if we are living what we are saying. The word *testimony* can mean far more than a brief flow of sentences. The word *testimony* can also describe the body of work that is our lives. May we live in such a way that people will mourn our dying and not our living.

There is no doubt that if we, as instructors, will attempt to walk as He walked, it will affect what we say and do, and we will positively impact the lives of others as a result. The challenge to develop the mind of Christ in the instructor is captured with great clarity by the songwriter who said, "Oh, to be like Thee, Blessed Redeemer. Oh, to be like Thee, pure as Thou art."

24

TIP #24

Happiness is the Child of Helpfulness

"For even the Son of man came not to be ministered unto, but to minister, and to give his life a ransom for many."
—Mark 10:45

One of the motifs of the Lancaster Baptist Church and West Coast Baptist College is that of "servant leadership." There is no doubt that John 13 (along with many other passages) shows the modeling of servant leadership by our Lord Jesus Christ.

Although service-oriented jobs are often looked down upon, and sometimes even despised, Christians need to understand the joy that comes from serving. One songwriter put it well when he said, "There is joy, joy, joy in serving Jesus." I do believe that this songwriter truly understood one of the deeper and more significant truths in the Christian life.

Instruction on having a servant's heart can bring about a life-changing result in the listener. Removing a "me-first" mentality and looking to prefer one another (Romans 12:10) is certainly the antithesis of the theme this world so often champions. In a culture that has become increasingly materialistic and heathenistic, the idea of serving is not usually welcomed with great applause. Yet, the student should experience the joy of putting others first, and ultimately experience what the Scripture teaches in Matthew 19:30: "*...many that are first shall be last; and the last shall be first.*" This principle of servant leadership will bring to fruition a fulfillment that the world knows little or nothing about.

True servanthood not only involves denying self, it also involves showing compassion for others. It is the servant leader who embodies the principle taught in Jude 22 which states, "*And of some have compassion, making a difference.*" This model, which was seen in the life of Washington at Valley Forge, Lincoln during the Civil War, Florence Nightingale during the Crimean War, and perhaps most auspiciously in the lives of untold thousands of Christian workers, truly embodies a Christ-likeness that will not only have a wide impact for today, but will also reap fruit for all eternity.

25

TIP #25

Every Choice Has a Consequence

"Be not deceived; God is not mocked: for whatsoever a man soweth, that shall he also reap."—Galatians 6:7

It is essential for mentors to help young people understand that the sowing of choices always brings a harvest of consequences. It is true that we harvest what we sow. It is also true that we always harvest *more* than we sow. A farmer who sows corn will grow a cornfield. The parent who sows a critical spirit will grow a critic.

When teaching on the importance of choices, it would be wise to share biblical principles, such as:

> "*...they have sown the wind, and they shall reap the whirlwind....*"—Hosea 8:7
>
> "*...it is appointed unto men once to die, but after this the judgment:*"—Hebrews 9:27
>
> "*...every one of us shall give account of himself to God.*" —Romans 14:12

It should also be understood that to achieve desired consequences, it would only be prudent to consider the steps necessary to achieve the desired result. This is true in many areas. If you desire to see souls saved, then an investment of time must be made to meet and follow-up on potential converts. If a student wants to excel in athletics, he may need to make personal sacrifices in order to grow in strength, speed, and understanding of the game. If we desire to become better Christians, we must read, memorize, and meditate on the Word of God.

In this moment, consider any choices that must be made in your life if you will reach your desired results. Then, identify ways in which you can encourage those you mentor to sow seeds that will reap beneficial consequences.

26

TIP #26

Education Is a Journey

"Till I come, give attendance to reading, to exhortation, to doctrine."—1 Timothy 4:13

As educators, we frequently talk about people acquiring an education. It is imperative for us to realize, however, that education is not just something we get; it is also something that we live.

Students, along with their teachers, must understand that growth and learning are lifelong processes. It has been said countless times that commencement is the beginning of education, not the closing of an instructional season. If students grasp this truth that learning is a journey, it will help them to continue growing on purpose. They may set goals for a lifelong reading plan, determine to develop a particular venue of life, or even memorize portions of God's Word.

We need to challenge students to be like Jesus Christ who, according to Luke 2:52, "*…increased in wisdom and stature, and in favour with God and man.*" We must challenge them to grow and increase in their knowledge, so they can be more effective for the Lord. John Gardner said, "We don't even know what skills may be needed in the years ahead. That is why we must train our young people in the fundamental fields of knowledge, and equip them to understand and cope with change. That is why we must give them the critical qualities of mind and durable qualities of character that will serve them in circumstances we cannot now even predict."

As teachers and students, we must comprehend that this journey is something that will continue until the Lord calls us home. We must understand that we can redeem the time and "occupy till He comes" through the process of personal growth and equipping others for service in the Lord's work.

27

TIP #27

"I Didn't Know" is Not a Valid Excuse

"So then every one of us shall give account of himself to God."—Romans 14:12

Perhaps, like me, you have had the experience of driving through an unfamiliar town when suddenly you realize you have just driven through a stop sign! Maybe you have visited another town and were not aware of the speed limit, but were instantly made aware of it by the flashing lights in your rearview mirror! Even the most casual observer would agree that telling the policeman, "I didn't know," in these types of situations is not usually a good enough argument to deter him from giving a ticket. When the IRS contacts a taxpayer regarding a problem on the tax return, the taxpayer's statement regarding his unawareness of the law will never suffice. "I didn't know," is not a valid excuse!

God has given us His Word in which His promises and commands are clearly stated. It is our responsibility to learn them and to apply them. Our failure to heed these principles will no more be excused at the Judgment Seat of Christ than will the speeder be excused by a judge because of his lack of knowledge of driving rules and regulations.

This truth should lead a mentor to do his best to create a thirst in the mind of the student to learn the principles and precepts that will help in proper decision making over a lifetime. Once this is accomplished, and the student begins to implement God's Word, then he has made a quantum leap in accepting responsibility to learn and acquire God's knowledge.

28

TIP #28

HELP NURTURES HOPE

"He restoreth my soul: he leadeth me in the paths of righteousness for his name's sake."—PSALM 23:3

When the child knows that his instructor's main interest is helping him become what he should, the response of the student will inevitably be affected.

The student needs to understand that the primary goal of the instructor is to help and to guide the student along a path that will bring growth. The Bible analogy is that of a shepherd who cares for his flock. The shepherd knows his flock. The shepherd knows when a sheep is missing. The shepherd is willing to go far beyond the "norm" to help that lost sheep make it. There should never be a doubt that the shepherd cares for the flock.

The instructor is there to help, encourage, and preserve. A student must understand and unquestionably realize that the instructor has the student's best interest at heart.

Finally, the student will understand that it is the dream—the hope—of the instructor to see the student enter the harvest fields of the Lord Jesus Christ.

29

TIP #29

HUMILITY OPENS HEARTS

"The meek will he guide in judgment: and the meek will he teach his way."—PSALM 25:9

"He must increase, but I must decrease."—JOHN 3:30

"These six things doth the Lord hate: yea, seven are an abomination unto him: A proud look...."—PROVERBS 6:16–17

People who come away from an encounter with a well-known public figure often discuss the pride that was evidently displayed. On the contrary, the Lord Jesus Christ modeled and taught us the principle of biblical humility. If we are to positively impact lives in the way that would please the Saviour, we must also model a humble spirit.

The instructor must understand that a humble spirit will open the heart of the student. Conversely, when the instructor speaks from a standpoint of pride (this could be pride of position or pride of preparation), it often serves as a hindrance to the learning process.

Instructors, we must remember that in and of ourselves dwells no good thing. We are blessed to be vessels in the hand of the Master. When we acknowledge this truth in our hearts, true humility is perceived and the student is more prone to listen to suggestions or to direction.

Our great example is the Lord Jesus Christ. Time and again He humbled Himself. Certainly, if the Lord Jesus Christ was willing to humble Himself, we ought to constantly seek "to die to self" and portray a humble and open spirit. We must not depend on ourselves to accomplish anything of long-term worth. We must utterly and completely depend on God.

Humility is not a denial of gifts or abilities, but rather recognition that true-life change can only come through the power of the Holy Spirit. It is an understanding that in all things, we need God.

30

TIP #30

How We Speak Is Almost as Important as What We Say

"A man hath joy by the answer of his mouth: and a word spoken in due season, how good is it!"—Proverbs 15:23

"Let your speech be alway with grace, seasoned with salt, that ye may know how ye ought to answer every man." —Colossians 4:6

In Proverbs 31:26, the virtuous woman demonstrates the correct way to speak—with wisdom and kindness. It would behoove instructors to remember these characteristics, as well as how they like to be spoken to when asked to complete a task. A harsh tone, a domineering spirit, or a caustic attitude all serve to close the heart to further instruction.

The Sunday school teacher would do well to emphasize this principle of godly speech. Although there are times when we are to "cry aloud" like the prophets of old, the students will usually be more receptive if the general tenor is one of helpfulness, compassion, and kindness that comes from a meek and humble spirit.

This principle should lead the instructor to think of the best way to phrase instruction. He should ask the Lord to show him the tone in which instruction should be given. This is also extraordinarily important in the life of the parent who is trying to *"train up a child in the way he should go"* (Proverbs 22:6).

Preparation by the teacher will help him as he prayerfully considers the best timing in which to convey truth. Consideration should be given to the time of the year and the time of the hour. Starting with a positive note will help the learning session get off to the right start. Closing with finality and summarization will help "wrap-up" a truth being conveyed.

The spirit, the tone, and the timing with which we speak are truly almost as important as the words we say. May our speech be gracious and uplifting!

31

TIP #31

Truths Wrapped in Stories Are More Easily Comprehended

"But without a parable spake he not unto them: and when they were alone, he expounded all things to his disciples." —Mark 4:34

"And he said unto them, Unto you it is given to know the mystery of the kingdom of God: but unto them that are without, all these things are done in parables:"—Mark 4:11

Jesus Christ spoke in parables! He used parable sayings, parable similitudes, and parable stories. Using these parable classifications, there are approximately sixty parables in the New Testament, with as many as eight found in a single chapter! Jesus Himself said, "*...I will open my mouth in parables*" (Matthew 13:35). The Bible says that Christ taught the people many things by using parables (Mark 4:2). (It was even prophesied that Jesus Christ would use parables to convey truth!)

According to Vine's dictionary, the primary meaning of the word *parable* is "a placing beside with a view to comparison."

For the instructor to effectively communicate, it is wise to place parables alongside truths or principles being taught. The Lord Jesus Christ used illustrations of things with which people were familiar in order to help them understand a principle that would help them in their daily lives.

People remember stories far longer than they remember outlines or lectures. Many great preachers of yesteryear were experts at telling stories that would resonate truth long after the speakers had passed from the scene. Perhaps you need to add stories and illustrations to your teaching style. Think of personal illustrations and research stories that will help people remember truths long after they forget your outline.

May we follow the example of Jesus as we seek to become more effective teachers for His glory!

32

TIP #32

Truths are Seeds to be Sown, Not Bullets to be Shot

"But speaking the truth in love, may grow up into him in all things, which is the head, even Christ:"—Ephesians 4:15

"O send out thy light and thy truth: let them lead me; let them bring me unto thy holy hill, and to thy tabernacles." —Psalm 43:3

At the heart of education is the understanding that truths will not bring about the desired effect until they have had time to germinate, sprout, and mature in the heart of the listener. Often, many years after their students graduate, instructors hear how their instruction wrought long-lasting benefits in the lives of those whom they taught.

Sometimes, people look for such an immediate change that the instruction tends to be badgering. Those involved in the training of livestock understand the word *gentling*. This is especially used when a horse is being broken to saddle and bridle. This principle is also applicable when we are trying to share truths that we hope to see come to fruition in the life of the student.

The instructor needs to look for truths that can be sown on each occasion of instruction. Great communicators have always looked to leave the student with one undeniable truth. The chances of this truth germinating and sprouting are far better if the instructor will not only share but will show the student the truth.

As these truths are taught, demonstrated, and then practiced, they will become a part of the life of the student. The adept instructor will be looking for ways to unobtrusively stamp these truths into lessons and lives.

33

TIP #33

Dreams or Themes—Discipline is the Means

"And every man that striveth for the mastery is temperate in all things. Now they do it to obtain a corruptible crown; but we an incorruptible."—1 Corinthians 9:25

There is always a price to be paid to achieve a desired goal. Although the concept of osmosis sounds intriguing and often makes us smile, it is not a realistic way to acquire learning, character, or growth. Oftentimes, people dream about what could have been done if only they had the initial discipline to do things differently. People do not accomplish great things for God by "chance."

Recently, I took part in a funeral of an 89-year-old woman of God who had taught Sunday school for decades. Many commented on what a tremendous Sunday school teacher she had been, so it did not surprise me when a friend of the family told me that anytime during the week, when an appearance was made at the Sanford home, one would find Mrs. Sanford preparing a Sunday school lesson for her children. She realized that the price entailed far more than fifteen minutes of preparation on a Saturday night or a quick glance at the lesson on Sunday morning. She was a woman of discipline.

When the Bible says that we are to put our hands to the plow, it is an obvious inference to labor. Young people must be taught that it is impossible to get to know God without spending time with Him. A price must be paid to grow in the areas of Bible reading, prayer, and personal study.

While we emphasize the importance of goals and strategies, discipline is required to see these become a reality. As teachers, we must discipline ourselves in the areas of study and personal growth. Next, we must commit to the investment of time that is required to make a difference in the lives of others. Then, we must show students the steps of discipline that will help their dreams and God's goals for their lives to become a reality.

34

TIP #34

You Can Only Lead in the Direction You Are Going

"Then said Jesus unto his disciples, If any man will come after me, let him deny himself, and take up his cross, and follow me."—Matthew 16:24

For instruction to take place, not only must students be mentored, but truths must be modeled. It is far easier to get people to a goal if we lead them along the path that will take them there. This enables us to point out potential pitfalls or rabbit trails along the way.

The Lord Jesus Christ was the Master Teacher, and He certainly modeled this Himself. He led by example. He showed us the true meaning of self sacrifice. He demonstrated what it meant to die to self, and displayed how to live for, reach out to, and care for others. He obediently forsook all to obey the Heavenly Father. The result of this perfect mentoring was that eleven men went on to turn the world upside down for the cause of Christ.

Jesus commanded His disciples to follow Him, so He could make them fishers of men. As they followed, Jesus showed them how to look for opportunities to reach out to others. Whether it was the woman with the issue of blood, blind Bartimaeus, Zacchaeus up in the tree, or Nicodemus at night, He modeled a sacrificial life as he demonstrated care for these and others. It is no surprise that this life of leadership was replicated in the lives of His followers.

35

TIP #35

Life is Like a Grindstone

"But he knoweth the way that I take: when he hath tried me, I shall come forth as gold."—Job 23:10

The grindstone of life can bring two very different responses from people. For some, the grindstone will refine them like the polished stone referred to in the Bible. Some, on the other hand, allow life to wear them down, and the grindstone removes their edge and diminishes their influence.

It has been said that the test of a man's character is what it takes to stop him. Instructors must teach the students to allow life's circumstances to grow them instead of causing them to quit—to make them better instead of bitter. Arthur Ward said that tribulation is a test tube. When difficulties occur, the student should learn to ask, "What can be learned from this?" "How can I grow as a result of this trial?" "What can I learn about God during this time of testing?"

It is important for the instructor to teach the student that difficulties are a part of life and that we are responsible for how we react to them and for what we learn from them.

It is the buffing cloth—with its repetitive actions—that brings out the deep shine in the shoe. For many, that "rubbing" is inconvenient and uncomfortable, but it is actually meant to polish, to shine, and to sharpen. Often, people will do everything in their power to avert the discomfort, which is the very thing meant to bring them to a polished state. Students should embrace the Father-filtered trials as opportunities to be sharpened for the glory of God.

36

TIP #36

PASSION PROPELS PERSUASION

"For I know the forwardness of your mind, for which I boast of you to them of Macedonia, that Achaia was ready a year ago; and your zeal hath provoked very many."
—2 CORINTHIANS 9:2

At the heart of every instructor is a desire to bring about change in the life of the student. Since there is an obvious understanding that change is necessary, we should ask, "How do we get the student to come to an understanding of the importance of the subject at hand?"

Passion in the instructor can help those under his sphere of influence and can persuade them to change. It was said of the Lord Jesus Christ that He did not speak as other men spoke; He possessed a passion to persuade like no one who has walked on this earth.

It would be a wonderful thing today if students would see a burning passion in the heart of the instructor—if they would see that the instructor was fully committed to the students' understanding and the living out of the truths being transferred.

It is understood by every administrator that the teachers who have a passion about their classes or subjects, are those who will truly be the difference makers. As in so many areas, if we are not passionate about what we teach, we should not expect our students to be persuaded or passionate about the material we share.

37

TIP #37

Wasting Time is Really Wasting Life

"Redeeming the time, because the days are evil."
—Ephesians 5:16

We all must understand that life is made up of time! How we spend our time determines how we spend our life.

Satan will do what he can to get us to spend our lives on that which is wrong and wasteful. One of the excuses he uses to get people to waste time is the act of procrastination. Procrastination not only puts off doing what is important, but it also eliminates productive time for later.

The instructor must teach the student that one of the great tools to avoid the wasting of time is to live by a schedule. God's Word teaches us to number our days. The student who learns that time spent in planning is some of the best use of time, will find that much less time will be wasted.

It is wise for the instructor to use analogies so that the student can understand the value of each day, week, month, and year. One such analogy is that life in many ways is like a game, and it has a finite number of minutes. Once those minutes are expended, they can never be retrieved. One author said that each week is filled with 168 golden hours, and once the sands of time pass through the hourglass, that golden hour can never be used; it can never be spent; and it can never be recaptured.

Finally, the instructor can help the student understand that, not only do we not know how much time we will have, but we will also give an account for how we spent our time. More time equals more accountability. With each day that passes, we have added to that for which we must give an account to the Lord.

38

TIP #38

The Road to Success is Always Under Construction

"But grow in grace, and in the knowledge of our Lord and Saviour Jesus Christ...."—2 PETER 3:18

One of the chief dangers for instructors and students alike is the danger of complacency. It cannot be overemphasized that as believers, we are to continue to grow in "*the nurture and admonition of the Lord*" (Ephesians 6:4).

The Christian life involves a transition and a maturation that entails growing from a baby Christian to an adult Christian. The Bible analogy is for those who are only able to take milk compared to those who are able to eat meat. The Apostle Paul illustrated this process of Christian growth when he stated at the close of his life that he had not "*attained*" (Philippians 3:12).

If the instructor can graft into the student the understanding that continued growth is not only wanted, but is a necessity, then this desire of the student can drive them to continue to be more like the Saviour.

The instructor needs to look for ways to perfect his teaching and become more efficient in the task which God has allowed him to do. There is always room for improvement. There is always a way to do a better job. There is always a way to be sharpened for the ministry that God has given. If we truly believe those statements, we will seek mentoring, continue growing, and seek change, although it is often uncomfortable.

39

TIP #39

Character is a Victory, Not a Gift

"But who may abide the day of his coming? and who shall stand when he appeareth? for he is like a refiner's fire...."
—Malachi 3:2

It is the incumbent responsibility of parents and teachers to work at the development of character in the life of the student. It is a false claim that some people have "just always had character." Character is something that is developed. The refinement of training is what equips the student for the difficult decisions that will be faced in the course of life. Since the instructor understands the trials, tribulations, and temptations that happen during life's journey, he must understand that the equipping of a student is of critical necessity in order to avoid failure in the future.

Character is only attained through effort from both the instructor and the student. This refining process could be compared to the combination of a fire and the ore. It is the fire that removes the impurities from the ore (Malachi 3:2). Without this fire, the dross will remain as a residual. This dross, which lessens the value of a precious metal, will lessen the effectiveness of a Christian servant. This development of character is what will form the student into the Christian God saved him to be.

Finally, it must be remembered that the development of character is never complete. Instructors would be wise to heed the words of a pastor, a spouse, or another friend who endeavors to tell him something whereby he will be sharpened. A good friend will endeavor to help us to do better and to be more effective in our service to the King.

Part 2

Things We Should Do

40

TIP #40

BE A VESSEL FIT FOR CHRIST

"Trust in the LORD with all thine heart; and lean not unto thine own understanding. In all thy ways acknowledge him, and he shall direct thy paths."—PROVERBS 3:5–6

When seeking to train and teach, we must realize our first priority is to be dependent upon the Lord. The Bible makes it clear that the arm of the flesh will fail us, but His arm fails not. Whether a parent or a teacher, it is of great importance to realize God is our source of wisdom and guidance.

It is a sad thing when frail humanity neglects the promise of help that is proffered from the Lord. The book of James says, "*If any of you lack wisdom, let him ask of God, that giveth to all men liberally, and upbraideth not; and it shall be given him*" (James 1:5).

Dr. John R. Rice was famous for saying, "We have not because we ask not." We need to rely on the Lord and trust in Him; He undoubtedly will lead us. Eleazar said in Genesis 24:27, "*...I being in the way, the Lord led me....*" It is a wonderful thing to know the Lord wants to lead us. It is solely up to us to ask Him for His help and guidance.

It all starts with our being vessels "fit for the Master's hand." As instructors seeking to influence a life for Christ and to instill Christ-likeness in the life of the hearer, we would do well to remember the words of Jeremiah 33:3, "*Call unto me, and I will answer thee, and shew thee great and mighty things, which thou knowest not.*"

41

TIP #41

Let Each Day Be a Clean Slate

"As far as the east is from the west, so far hath he removed our transgressions from us."—Psalm 103:12

Everyone likes to have a fresh start. There is no question that sin must be dealt with and mistakes corrected. Unfortunately, however, we often remember failures, faults, mistakes, and transgressions far more quickly than we remember kindness, obedience, and adherence to mandated protocols.

True forgiveness, at its zenith, involves forgetting. Our Heavenly Father remembers our sins no more. We do not have this ability to forget mistakes and transgressions, but we must remember that for the good of the party involved, once the issue has been addressed and dealt with, it should not be brought up again. While we cannot forget, we can decide not to bring it up again.

The pristine beauty and hope of the new day should be available to every child. The day should be greeted with hope and not dread. When the day begins with a clean start, the student can understand that while failure may have occurred the previous day, today can be a day of victory.

A parallel that most adults would understand is how we often view the start of a new year. It is a time when new promises are made, old habits are done away with, and new habits are established. It is a turning over of a new leaf. This same concept can be applied on a daily basis with the instructor holding up the promise of hope for the child. One must remember that we tend to enjoy things at which we succeed. It is for this reason that once judgment has been passed and punishment meted out, we need to move on to a fresh start.

42

TIP #42
Ask for Help

"Without counsel purposes are disappointed: but in the multitude of counsellors they are established."—Proverbs 15:22

"Hear counsel, and receive instruction, that thou mayest be wise in thy latter end."—Proverbs 19:20

"For by wise counsel thou shalt make thy war: and in multitude of counsellors there is safety."—Proverbs 24:6

"Many hands make the burden light." While I would tend to vehemently disagree with the "it takes a village..." concept espoused by Mrs. Clinton, I think it is both obvious and true that the more help that can be garnered in the teaching process, the more effective the whole process will be. The principle of one slaying 1,000 and two slaying 10,000 is still true.

The Bible clearly states in Ecclesiastes 4:12 that "*...a threefold cord is not quickly broken.*" I believe this threefold cord could symbolize the family, the church, and the school co-laboring together.

One of the critical elements involved in getting help for children or students is to be sure they understand that the teacher and parent have a high degree of respect for others who are involved in the teaching process. One of the most grievous things that can happen in the training of a young person is to hear a pastor or schoolteacher criticized by the parent. Likewise, the homes should not be criticized in the classroom. This makes it very difficult for the student to respect those from whom they should be getting counsel.

A major mistake that must be avoided is thinking that the primary instructor has every answer in dealing with the student. It is wise for parents and teachers to communicate with each other and to ask for help, so they can determine the best way to aid in a particular learning process.

43

TIP #43
Choose Your Battles Wisely

"Behold, how good and how pleasant it is for brethren to dwell together in unity!"—Psalm 133:1

The instructor, whether at home or in the classroom, is often faced with potential conflicts. I had the privilege of growing up in a home that was remarkably free of strife between my parents and siblings, which included six headstrong boys! It was amazing how clearly we understood that our parents were in charge and that authority was not to be questioned or challenged. (Although, as is often the case, as teenagers, we did not always do what our parents expected us to do. There was a minimum amount of overt rebellion and even disagreement!)

In all probability, this peaceful environment might have been due to parents who decided to choose their battles wisely. Some battles were clearly delineated, such as personal standards regarding refraining from smoking and drinking, single dating, or being alone in a house with a member of the opposite gender.

On the other hand, there were small issues one might call "nonessential." These were not treated as the "Laws of the Medes and Persians." Some battles parents might not want to fight are the choice of hairstyle on a young man that would be biblical in length, but maybe not the style the father would have or a type of shoe or clothing that would not be our choice, but would not be wrong.

The critical component is to make sure the student understands exactly what is truly important to the instructor. It is also imperative that the student understands that if one goes outside the clearly stated bounds, there will be "*mega*" consequences that exceed the pleasure of willful disobedience.

If it is important for the instructor to win the battle (and it is) then it might be wise to decide beforehand exactly what the battles should be.

44

TIP #44

Search for the Good

"And he shall sit as a refiner and purifier of silver: and he shall purify the sons of Levi, and purge them as gold and silver, that they may offer unto the Lord an offering in righteousness."—Malachi 3:3

As I write this book, precious metals are going through a lengthy and substantial period of appreciation. Among the most precious of these metals is gold. It astounded me to find out how little an amount of gold is actually in a ton of refined ore. Upon learning this, it became apparent that in the great majority of cases, the actual gold ore is an infinitesimal percentage of the total amount of earth that is moved. It also became apparent that the successful gold miners are always looking for the gold, the glitter, or that narrow vein (which may be only the width of a pencil lead) residing in loose sand. These small percentages do add up to be of great value.

The teacher needs to look for the glittering gold as well. The good needs to be encouraged and drawn out. Oftentimes, we are so overcome by the vast areas that need help, that we fail to notice that which is precious in the life of the student. It is that "precious" characteristic in a student that can be developed and refined into something of great value. This type of life will often be known for its quality and endurance resulting in causing the instructor to forget the arduous teaching process.

When you look at your students or your children, what do you see? Do you see a loud, impetuous, over-eager fisherman, or do you see a faithful, loving servant, who, empowered by God, would be used to preach at Pentecost? Ask God to help you look for the good in the lives of those you teach.

45

TIP #45

Major on Truth Not Trivia

"I will worship toward thy holy temple, and praise thy name for thy lovingkindness and for thy truth: for thou hast magnified thy word above all thy name."—Psalm 138:2

John 17:17 says, "*Sanctify them through thy truth: thy word is truth.*" The word *sanctify* means "to set apart." It is truth that brings about substantive changes in the life of the student and sets them apart for the work of the Lord. Much of the intellectual trivia, thought processes, and language patterns that occupy our daily lives has little or no effect on the heart. The Word of God teaches us that the way people are truly set apart as chosen vessels is through the truth of God's Word.

Although there is a place for humor and interesting anecdotes, the instructor must remember that it is the **truth** of God's Word that pierces and divides asunder. It is the **truth** of God's Word that shows a young man how to cleanse his way. It is the **truth** of God's Word that helps us not to sin against God. It is the **truth** of God that is a lamp unto our feet and a light unto our path.

There is no doubt that God gave us Psalm 119 to show us the importance He places on the **truth** of His Word. It is the **truth** of God's Word that He has set above His own name. It is because of this that the instructor teaching Sunday school or a Bible class, or the parent instructing in the home, needs to concentrate on the most important transference of all... the transfer of the **truth** of God's Word to the heart of the student.

Sir Walter Scott, while lying on his deathbed, asked his servant to bring him a book. The servant replied, "Sir Walter, you have thousands of books."

Scott responded, "But at a time like this, there is only one Book. Bring me the Bible." Scott had understood that it was not a time for trivia but a time for the **truth** of God's Word.

46

TIP #46
Cast a Vision

"And he saith unto them, Follow me, and I will make you fishers of men."—Matthew 4:19

The Lord Jesus Christ not only saw a fisherman named Peter, but he saw a man who would ultimately be used to move men and change lives for the cause of Christ. One of the primary purposes of a teacher is to create a vision in the lives of the students, to help the students see themselves the way the Lord Jesus Christ sees them. They need to see that they can be "*a vessel…meet for the master's use.*"

When it comes to casting vision, we are to be in the commissioning, as well as in the commending process. Every instructor ought to inspire Christ-likeness and Christian service in the heart of the student. A child overhearing the prayers of a parent, a student receiving a note from a mentor, an instructor visualizing what a student may do for the cause of Christ, a teacher writing a note of encouragement on a paper telling the student he should use his gift of preaching or teaching to serve the Lord—each of these experiences can create a vision in the heart of a student for what God can do in his life.

God's Word says, "*Where there is no vision, the people perish…*" (Proverbs 29:18). The instructors of today need to be the vision casters for the leaders of tomorrow. Create a vision in your students that reaches for the stars. Teach them to dream big for God and His purpose for their lives; "*For with God nothing shall be impossible*" (Luke 1:37).

47

TIP #47

Develop Godly Friendships

"A friend loveth at all times, and a brother is born for adversity."—Proverbs 17:17

"Iron sharpeneth iron; so a man sharpeneth the countenance of his friend."—Proverbs 27:17

One of the great concerns of nearly every individual, whether in the home, church, or school, is that of developing friendships. In a world that puts tremendous emphasis on seeking friendships through fulfilling personal ambition, the Christian must understand that true friendship was best modeled by the Lord Jesus Christ, who sought to be a Friend to others (Proverbs 18:24). It was He who loved without being loved in return and forgave before apologies were offered. How true are the words penned by the songwriter, John Chapman, when he wrote, *Jesus, What a Friend for Sinners.* This man understood the true friendship we find in Christ.

It is the instructor's job to strive to be a friend to those he is mentoring. (For the young instructor, it is necessary to remember there is a difference between being a friend and being a "buddy.") A true friend does not let another friend make mistakes if it can be helped. A true friend is willing to correct someone when it is in his best interest. A true friend focuses on the needs of others and not on his own needs. A true friend is a valuable resource and an unusual commodity in the world in which we live.

Like so many other principles in life, this lesson of godly friendship is best learned when modeled. Are you displaying true friendship to those you influence? May we all understand the great value of helping students learn the true meaning of friendship.

48

TIP #48
CREATE TEACHABLE MOMENTS

"And thou shalt teach them diligently unto thy children, and shalt talk of them when thou sittest in thine house, and when thou walkest by the way, and when thou liest down, and when thou risest up."—DEUTERONOMY 6:7

Can you stop and reflect on that special teacher you had either in school or in a Sunday school class? I recently had the privilege of calling up my fourth and fifth grade teacher who now resides in New York. I still thrill to hear the joy in the voice of this 66-year-old lady, who is now battling cancer, and reflect on her time of teaching the fourth and fifth grades in a Christian school. I have told listeners across the country how Mrs. Prehmus made my elementary life come alive. She often read to us, introduced us to authors and titles, played exciting games with us, and did many other things to make class fun and interesting. She became one of my most memorable teachers.

Oftentimes, the memories that are created come from capturing that teachable moment. Other times, it is finding just the right illustration, visual aid, quote to buttress a well-planned lecture, a personal visit, a lunch, a special note, a phone call, or an article or book sent to the student that deals with his field of interest.

Memories are also created through the sharing and spending of time. The instructor must understand that these quality moments are often an outgrowth of quality time. The best memories are usually the times we spent with people, rather than the things we have purchased for them. As a parent, it might be staying up late to talk, bringing in an unexpected cup of hot chocolate, mailing a letter from another address for your child to receive at home, putting a little note in a lunchbox, or taking a child out for a surprise excursion about which they had no idea. While we may not be able to perform a memory-maker on a daily basis, it would be wise for the instructor to think each week, "What can I do this week to create a teachable moment?"

49

TIP #49

LEARN FROM YOUR STUDENTS

"If I then, your Lord and Master, have washed your feet; ye also ought to wash one another's feet. For I have given you an example, that ye should do as I have done to you. Verily, verily, I say unto you, The servant is not greater than his lord; neither he that is sent greater than he that sent him."—JOHN 13:14–16

The adage that "Every man is my teacher" is applicable not solely with the hoary-headed. Sometimes the younger generation, whether our students or our children, can teach us ways to improve, connect, or help them in more thorough and fulfilling ways. We can learn from and listen to those who are in our watch care in many ways: such as noticing if they are tired or alert, listening or lethargic, disinterested or involved.

A second and third grade math teacher once said, "A teacher who listens to the ideas of their students is a teacher who continues to learn."

Above all, we need to learn from our students when we ask them questions. While asking questions is a great teaching method, it is also a phenomenal tool to decipher the extent to which understanding is being achieved. By learning where your students are in their comprehension, you will know whether to speed up, slow down, or clarify truths that are needed before progressing to the next subject of study. It is a horrible mistake to treat students as inanimate objects, sitting there solely as aural receptors of the truths and principles we are trying to share.

If we are going to learn from our students, we need to watch them, listen to them, and ask them questions. After we have ascertained the level of understanding and interest, we must then adapt to the situation at hand.

50

TIP #50

Don't Do for Your Students What They Could Do for Themselves

"Teach me, O Lord, the way of thy statutes; and I shall keep it unto the end."—Psalm 119:33

"Now therefore perform the doing of it; that as there was a readiness to will, so there may be a performance also out of that which ye have."—2 Corinthians 8:11

"That the man of God may be perfect, throughly furnished unto all good works."—2 Timothy 3:17

Second Timothy 2:2 states, "*And the things that thou hast heard of me among many witnesses, the same commit thou to faithful men, who shall be able to teach others also.*"

This can start as early as when a parent understands that he can make a bed far more quickly than a young child. However, there is an incalculable lesson that is missed when the work is done for them.

Once an explanation has been given and students are allowed to solve the problems on their own, there is a sense of victory and accompanying vitality that gives tremendous power to the learning process. It is a great danger to overly critique or criticize the early stages of the learning process. This may discourage students from even trying to succeed or accomplish something on their own.

To some extent, this is teaching the students to step out by faith, to enter the unknown, and to try on their own. Victory comes with accomplishment.

51

TIP #51

Involve Multiple Senses in the Learning Process

"But as it is written, Eye hath not seen, nor ear heard, neither have entered into the heart of man, the things which God hath prepared for them that love him."—1 Corinthians 2:9

God gave us five senses that work together in order to give awareness and understanding of the world around us. If one's eyes were tightly banded shut and his nose plugged before given a bite of a raw slice of onion, he would most likely think it to be an apple. However, when the tingling of the eyes and the pungency of the aroma of the freshly cut onion is combined with the effect of the taste buds, there is an unmistakable result for the person eating the onion!

When the instructor involves more than one sense, he can more effectively transfer a principle or truth. Therefore, he must look over the material to see what descriptions, illustrations, and aids can be used to encourage the listener to involve multiple senses. Although a lecture largely involves hearing, it is important to paint a picture that one can see with the mental eye. If sight and sound could be seen and heard through the halls of one's imagination, it would force the memory to be more deeply entrenched and less likely to be forgotten.

Many will never forget certain smells associated with their grandmother's house, the sounds of Christmas, or the sight of certain loved ones. The instructor needs to ask, "What smells, sights, and sounds will be recollected when the lecture notebook has been closed, the lights turned off, and the student pillows his head at the end of the day?"

52

TIP #52

Encourage Curiosity

"Then I saw, and considered it well: I looked upon it, and received instruction."—Proverbs 24:32

"For Ezra had prepared his heart to seek the law of the Lord, *and to do it, and to teach in Israel statutes and judgments."* —Ezra 7:10

"We will not hide them from their children, shewing to the generation to come the praises of the Lord, *and his strength, and his wonderful works that he hath done."*—Psalm 78:4

While it has often been said, "Curiosity killed the cat," the instructor must remember the active mind is a questioning mind. When questioning takes place, learning is often occurring.

The incredible curiosity of a young child is highly connected to the fact that a vast majority of basic understanding takes place between the ages of two and six. Every parent remembers the unending questions that seem to proliferate from the mouths and minds of preschool children. Yet each question, "Why?" or cry for explanation was merely the mental process by which facts and understanding were being assimilated.

Rather than quenching curiosity, the instructor must do everything in his power to encourage people to ask "What if?" "Why?" "What are the results?" "How does this apply to me?"

The cultivation of questions and curiosity must be a goal of the instructor. This is the antithesis of one who speaks, not wondering or caring about the degree of receptivity on the part of the listener. The development of curiosity and the encouraging of questions will also enable the instructor to constantly make minor adjustments in both the pace of the lesson given, as well as in the degree of explanation.

Finally, when curiosity is truly developed to its full maturation, it will give the listener the desire to continue to learn and grow beyond what was covered during that single teaching moment. Questions will be asked of others, books will be read, and thoughts will be developed because the soil of the student's mind has been broken open by the plow of curiosity, leaving a fertile field ripe for learning.

53

TIP #53

Encourage Dreams but Value Action

"But where are thy gods that thou hast made thee? let them arise, if they can save thee in the time of thy trouble: for according to the number of thy cities are thy gods, O Judah."—Jeremiah 2:28

"I have also spoken by the prophets, and I have multiplied visions, and used similitudes, by the ministry of the prophets."—Hosea 12:10

We live in a world today that constantly encourages people to have big dreams, yet many times teachers or parents belittle their students' or children's dreams. The Word of God clearly states in Proverbs 29:18, "*Where there is no vision, the people perish....*"

It is important to encourage students to dream big for God and to follow the God-given vision for their lives. Repeatedly, however, there is a malaise of going beyond the initial stage of vision and entering into a stage of productivity. Society seems to crown the procrastinator with plaudits, as long as he has an idea for the future. In contrast, the instructor must help the student understand that the rest of his academic, physical, and spiritual life starts today.

Action must be taken right away! Instructors need to be proactive in getting young people started on projects. We must be concerned about helping the next generation develop a daily walk with the Lord, a regular time for witnessing and outreach, a time for a personal reading program, a methodical plan for Bible memory, as well as a plan for physical health and well-being.

Luke 2:52 states, "*And Jesus increased in wisdom and stature, and in favour with God and man.*" This verse could be an outline for the instructor to use in helping the listener open new venues in his life. A teacher should constantly seek for ways to "jump start" the student into areas of growth and godliness that are not already habitual in the life of the student.

54

TIP #54

Praise Publicly, Reprimand Privately

"Withhold not good from them to whom it is due, when it is in the power of thine hand to do it."—Proverbs 3:27

Whenever possible, the instructor should do everything within his power to encourage and praise where others can hear and then use one-on-one correction. Perhaps it would behoove the teacher to remember times in his life in which he experienced unnecessary embarrassment. The pain and the attitudinal changes that often accompany such reprimands, usually outweigh the benefit of the moments.

Admittedly, there are times when correction must be done instantaneously, and there is no recourse other than to correct someone in front of the class or siblings. In order to follow up on this principle, however, it is best to first make a general correction in class prior to naming individuals.

On the other side of the coin, public praise not only encourages the one who has done well, but it also acts as an inspiration for others who are listening. Much behavior that is done in society today is done for the purpose of garnering attention. Wrong actions can often be attributed to peer pressure and a desire for acceptance. So, the teacher should strive to provide that attention and acceptance through public praise before rules are broken by a disruptive student.

Sometimes, all a student needs for his heart to be brought to repentance is a reminder of the timely words spoken by a caring teacher. When Peter denied Christ, the mere remembrance of his Master's teaching, which occurred upon the crowing of the cock, was enough to bring him to a state of sorrow and remorse for his sin.

It ought to be the goal of the instructor to constantly be praising and encouraging the student. Remember the important principle found in Proverbs 16:21 that states, "*...the sweetness of the lips increaseth learning.*"

55

TIP #55

Edify through Emulation

"Those things, which ye have both learned, and received, and heard, and seen in me, do: and the God of peace shall be with you."—Philippians 4:9

A small handful of men turned the world upside-down. We know these men as the apostles of the Lord Jesus Christ. What they did baffles the imagination some two thousand years later. All—except John, who died in exile on the island of Patmos—died martyrs' deaths. Yet, they left legacies that effectuated unparalleled change in human history.

Why? How? I believe it is because they had the Master Teacher in all of history to emulate. In Matthew 4:19, it was the Lord Jesus Christ who said, "*...Follow me, and I will make you fishers of men.*" Truly, they were willing to follow Him.

Whether a parent or a teacher, we must understand the importance of finding good role models, learning from them, and even emulating them. Questions need to be raised, such as, "What have they done that has brought about success?" "How did they bring about change in their students' lives?" "How was character incorporated or transferred to their students?" Once these questions are answered, it would be wise to copy them. Although no two situations are the same, we can learn from those who have preceded us.

As a teacher, think about those teachers who impacted you. Look for examples of those who were best at making a lesson interesting, showing love for a class, or giving extra time to invest in his students. Seek to emulate the one who cared about the heart, the one who modeled a Christian walk, or the one who inspired you to follow Christ. Then, attempt to do the same things in the generation that God has placed in your hands.

56

TIP #56

Go above the Expectation

"What shall I render unto the Lord *for all his benefits toward me?"*—Psalm 116:12

"A man's gift maketh room for him, and bringeth him before great men."—Proverbs 18:16

The rhetorical question posed by the Lord Jesus Christ in Matthew 5:47 ought to provoke all of those who are trying to impact the lives of others. Jesus asked the question, *"And if ye salute your brethren only, what do ye more than others…?"*

Today we live in a world in which mediocrity is not only common, it is celebrated. What a disturbing thought that most people seem to be happy to find the lowest common denominator and attach themselves to it. On the contrary, we know God is pleased with excellent work, since His Word states in Psalm 16:3 that His delight is in the excellent. We must train students to find out what is expected of them and then go beyond that expectation.

Challenges need to be made regarding a personal walk, a heart for others, academic excellence, a desire to prepare one's self, spirit, and attitude, and a myriad of other areas. They must be encouraged to go beyond the norms of today's society or even the family.

It is highly important for the student to understand and realize there are some basic expectations God has for every believer. These, of course, would include Bible study, prayer, soulwinning, giving, and serving. The question then must be posed, "Are your students willing to go above the general basics of what could be called 'baseline Christianity'?"

This is a primary area in which the instructor must be engaged in goal setting. It is true that "one who aims at nothing hits it every time," and the challenge must be created for the student to strive for excellence.

57

TIP #57

Accentuate Solutions

"He that handleth a matter wisely shall find good: and whoso trusteth in the Lord, happy is he."—Proverbs 16:20

"A prudent man foreseeth the evil, and hideth himself: but the simple pass on, and are punished."—Proverbs 22:3

One of the primary problems pervasive in our society today is the defeatist attitude which emphasizes societal ills, failures, and difficulties. Leaders in the church, school, and home are the problem solvers. These are the ones who will not allow problems to defeat them, but rather will find a way to overcome them.

Leaders are by their very nature, problem solvers. And today, in our homes and schools, we need to make it a primary goal to train up leaders for the next generation. While there is always a place for one who takes a problem to a superior for help, advice, and solutions, it is of far greater benefit if one can help in the solution process.

If one can learn to find the problem and then look for potential solutions prior to bringing it to the parent or teacher, it would create an incalculable value in the life of that student.

The teacher can accomplish this goal by explaining how a particular problem could have been avoided in the first place. He could show how to arrive at different solutions by properly chosen previous decisions. This would necessitate choosing the right path in order to get to the right decision.

God's Word says in Psalm 37:23, "*The steps of a good man are ordered by the Lord....*" By following God's order many problems will ultimately be avoided.

58

TIP #58

Plan Thoroughly Then Follow Through

"For which of you, intending to build a tower, sitteth not down first, and counteth the cost, whether he have sufficient to finish it?" —Luke 14:28

At Lancaster Baptist Church, I have often heard the phrase, "He who fails to plan, plans to fail." The use of predetermined checkpoints, the calendaring of ideas, and a daily planning time are steps that can help the student be both more efficient and more effective in his daily life.

Unfortunately, in the society in which we now live, decisions are often made based on the "tyranny of the urgent." Furthermore, in the lives of young people, decisions are not usually based on long-term effects or results, but rather on the desires of the moment. The great philosopher of yesteryear, Dr. Bob Jones, Sr., stated that we are not to sacrifice the permanent on the altar of the immediate.

We need to be looking to the future to what God would have us do, thinking as to how we can prepare. Once this preparation has been made, it is of the utmost importance to activate the times and means so the plans can be brought to fruition. The man who built his house on the sand in Matthew 7 did not plan thoroughly, and the man in Luke 14:28–30 who began building the house but did not have enough money to finish it, did not plan thoroughly. The virgins spoken of in Matthew 25:1–5, did not have any oil when the bridegroom came, and they did not plan thoroughly.

While the Bible clearly teaches the importance of effective planning, we must also make sure the student is willing to follow through and complete the task ahead.

59

TIP #59

Cultivate Reverence Toward God

"Who is like unto thee, O Lord, among the gods? who is like thee, glorious in holiness, fearful in praises, doing wonders?"—Exodus 15:11

"Speak unto all the congregation of the children of Israel, and say unto them, Ye shall be holy: for I the Lord your God am holy."—Leviticus 19:2

"Thou shalt sanctify him therefore; for he offereth the bread of thy God: he shall be holy unto thee: for I the Lord, which sanctify you, am holy."—Leviticus 21:8

In a Christian environment, in most cases, the student will readily admit he believes in God. However, is there truly a respect and reverence for God, the Creator of the universe, the Saviour of the world? *American Heritage* magazine talks about brushes with history. It tells a story in each issue about how someone has had his life intersect or interact with someone of historical note or importance. Many times, this single encounter will have a profound effect on a person's life. The instructor must develop a heart attitude in the student to continually seek encounters with God.

Society has become so casual in its treatment of authority that this has inadvertently leaped into our theology. The Bible says that God is *the Alpha and Omega, the first and the last*. In Luke 11, the model prayer teaches us that we are to say, "*Hallowed be thy name.*" This same prayer teaches us that we are to seek God's will to be done on earth as much as it is done in Heaven. This is a reverential, respectful attitude toward the One who rules the universe.

There is no question that when the attitude toward our *Creator* is correct, it will help our attitude toward His *creation* to be correct. The classic book by Sheldon, *In His Steps*, attempted to portray a town that was captivated by asking the question, "What would Jesus do?" This question elevated and cultivated a reverence toward God.

A beautiful illustration of reverencing God is found in studying the Puritan life in early American history. You can see it in books such as *The History of the Plymouth Plantation* by William Bradford. Our early forefathers truly sought God's will and direction in each and every facet of their lives.

When the student starts to realize and understand the attributes of God, including His omnipotence, omniscience, and omnipresence, there will undoubtedly be a healthy respect that will affect daily choices, attitudes, and actions.

60

TIP #60

Teach the Acceptance of Responsibility

"He that covereth his sins shall not prosper: but whoso confesseth and forsaketh them shall have mercy."
—Proverbs 28:13

One of the hallmarks of our society today is the rapidity with which a person, under accusation or correction, will attempt to blame-shift that for which he is being corrected. One of the cardinal goals when using the Romans Road, for instance, is to get people to admit they are sinners. Yet, while we all acknowledge and understand we are sinners, most people would like to believe they are not too bad. If we can teach responsibility for actions, this will affect response to authority in all venues of life. It is a wonderful thing when someone says, "I'm sorry, I was wrong. You were right; Please forgive me," after being corrected. Unfortunately, excuses are usually given instead.

Part of what we are trying to teach, whether in the school classroom, Sunday school classroom, or the home, is the principle of responsibility. The easy way is always to blame someone else. This is not a new sin habit. In fact, we saw this take place in the Bible as far back as Genesis 3. First, Adam blamed his sin on Eve (Genesis 3:12), then, the woman quickly transferred the blame to the serpent (Genesis 3:13).

The instructor needs to disallow excuses and force the student to admit culpability or guilt. The worse possible situation would be to allow these excuses to slide and to make allowance for mistakes. If a Bible was not brought to Sunday school class, it is no one's fault other than the one who forgot the Bible. If a homework assignment was not turned in, blame should not be placed on any one of the inventive, creative circumstances that are often used.

Children and students need to be taught to take responsibility for their actions.

61

TIP #61

USE GROUP GOALS

"And he said, Come with me, and see my zeal for the LORD*...."*—2 KINGS 10:16

One of the mottos of our ministry at Lancaster Baptist Church and West Coast Baptist College is, "Teamwork makes the dream work." The student must understand the importance of synergy and the power and importance of the body as a whole. This principle, when taught, can make an enormous difference in a classroom, a family, or a Sunday school class. When a class is given a Scripture memory goal for instance, everyone should be exhorted to pursue it. Sometimes the slower individual is helped by the progress and influence of the class as a whole.

Race car drivers who use the technique called *drafting*, illustrate this in a unique way. When a race car gets close enough to the car in front of it, the air that is being broken by the lead car will flow over the second car, thus making it much easier for the second car to conserve fuel and maintain a close proximity to the lead car. In effect, as the air flows over the two cars, it is almost as if they are locked together.

This progress can occur in a class as well. In early American history, the method was called the Lancastrian Movement. This was necessitated by the one-room schoolhouse. A teacher would inspire the top students to mentor students who were slower or younger in order to achieve the common goal of the entire student body going forward.

Goals could be set spiritually, socially, mentally, and physically for the group or class as a whole. This could be seen in attendance goals, offering goals, reading goals, or even in the achievement of increase in a score average.

The Word of God makes it clear in, 1 Corinthians 12, that each part of the body has its own individual importance and all of the parts work together for the good of the body as a whole. So incorporate group goals and encourage teamwork as you train the next generation.

62

TIP #62

Being Proactive and Not Reactive

"A prudent man foreseeth the evil, and hideth himself: but the simple pass on, and are punished."—Proverbs 22:3

Many years ago, I heard someone state, "Some people make things happen, some people watch things happen, and some people wonder what happened." Although the phrase may be somewhat simplistic, I think there is more than just a little truth to this statement. We must be proactive and not reactive. We must decide that we are going to make things happen in the classroom and in the home, rather than just allow things to happen.

Science has taught us that things left to themselves do not get better. They deteriorate, they degenerate, and eventually, they cease to have value. As teachers and mentors, we cannot sit back and watch what happens when we leave children to themselves. We must be proactively involved in their lives so they will not degenerate educationally and spiritually.

The most important principle to understand in being proactive is that proactive people focus on using principles and root reasons to bring about a certain behavior. A reactive instructor will concentrate solely on the fruit or the action that is seen in a particular situation. A wise instructor will realize that a fruit problem is almost always indicative of a root problem.

Are we urging the students to have a heart for God? Are we urging them to seek God first? Are we urging them to honor God in all they do? This proactive behavior must be a goal within the heart of the instructor.

63

TIP #63

Inspire to Learn

"Study to shew thyself approved unto God, a workman that needeth not to be ashamed, rightly dividing the word of truth."—2 Timothy 2:15

True teaching does not just involve giving of knowledge, but also creating and stimulating (in the mind of the student) a desire to learn and accumulate knowledge and understanding for himself.

Some instructors have been prone to say that you can lead the student to learn, but you cannot force a student to learn. While that statement is true, one must understand that it is important to inspire students to want to learn. You cannot force a horse to drink water, but you can put salt in his oats to make him thirsty.

So, what can we do to create a thirst that will inspire a student to learn? The answer lies in the use of different teaching methodology. Going beyond the lecture can help stretch the mind and the imagination. It is often good to take the student past his comfort zone, whether incorporating play acting, using the question as a teaching method, creating a visual aid, or procuring a book or article for students to read. All of these tools might help awaken a thirst which may not already exist.

John Wesley, while writing his nephew, John Trenbeth, stated that, perhaps by beginning to read, he could acquire a taste that he had not acquired by that time. It was Wesley's desire for his nephew to begin to learn and to love books in the same way he did. While Trenbeth may never have ridden a horse for thousands of miles while resting a book on the pommel horn of his saddle, he might have set aside some time for daily devotional study that would help him in the ministry to which God had appointed him. John Wesley inspired him to learn.

It is the instructor's job to bring about the epiphany, the awakening, of interest that might seemingly be very far below the subconscious, in order to start the student on a new road of understanding and learning.

64

TIP #64

Focus on the Students

"Be thou diligent to know the state of thy flocks, and look well to thy herds."—Proverbs 27:23

Good instructors constantly watch the student to gauge his progress. Sometimes, an instructor can be so caught up in his schedule, problems, interests, or even personal passions that he forgets that teaching is transference of knowledge.

There are a number of factors for which the instructor must look as he focuses on the student. One of the easiest ways to tell how the student is doing is to frequently try to make eye contact. (However, the instructor must realize that when the gaze of a student is fixed and unblinking, the student is probably closer to comatose than concentration!)

Giving frequent quizzes over the material is another tool that can be used to monitor the progress of the students. In a Sunday school or home Bible study arena, this is accomplished by asking questions. It is a major misconception that questions must always be placed at the end of a lecture. Sometimes questions used throughout the lecture will have a higher degree of efficiency. Questions also allow the instructor to know whether the understanding has progressed, has stalled, or in a worst-case scenario, has not even begun to break above the surface of the student's consciousness.

It is extremely important for a parent or teacher to focus on the student! This involves interaction, questioning, and testing. It is imperative to know where a given student is on his academic journey and then to encourage him to take the next step.

65

TIP #65
ELIMINATE DISTRACTIONS

"Ye shall observe to do therefore as the LORD your God hath commanded you: ye shall not turn aside to the right hand or to the left."—DEUTERONOMY 5:32

"Brethren, I count not myself to have apprehended: but this one thing I do, forgetting those things which are behind, and reaching forth unto those things which are before."—PHILIPPIANS 3:13

"Wherefore seeing we also are compassed about with so great a cloud of witnesses, let us lay aside every weight, and the sin which doth so easily beset us, and let us run with patience the race that is set before us,"—HEBREWS 12:1

An instructor must realize that there will never be a perfect learning environment this side of Heaven. Be that as it may, it is still the instructor's job to try to remove distractions that will lessen the effectiveness, or even make ineffectual the learning process.

There are two major types of distractions that can affect the student. The first of these distractions is an internal distraction. This is when a student is thinking about something else.

The instructor needs to teach the student that, when some important thoughts come to mind the student needs to write them down and go back to them at another time when he can do something about the problem.

How many times have we, as adults, been faced with an issue such as, "Did we pay the bills?" or "Did we remember to call a friend?" These are relevant and important, but they can distract us from the issue that is at hand. The best possible solution is to take out a 3 x 5 card, write that down, and then, at a pre-appointed time, go over the thoughts and questions that need to be dealt with that day.

The second type of distraction that needs to be eliminated is the external distraction. In a classroom, this could be an open window through which the noise of the playing children nearby could affect the student. It could be a television in the home, a radio broadcast, a picture on a desk, or a communication with someone who is in the same room.

Many times I have encouraged one of my children to go into a different room away from the family and shut the door in order to eliminate the external distraction.

When these distractions, both internal and external, are eliminated, learning becomes easier and more efficient.

66

TIP #66

Admit Weaknesses, but Don't Accept Them

"And he saith unto them, Follow me, and I will make you fishers of men."—Matthew 4:19

The person who claims to be perfect or acts as if he has no room for growth is making a great error. It is only proper and correct for students, and instructors, alike to *admit* a weakness. However, the critical decision must be made not to *accept* the admitted weakness.

We all know the areas in which we need help—for some it is with diet and exercise, for others it is in a dedicated walk with the Lord, and others it might be in the area of personal soulwinning. It is an excellent first step to acknowledge an area that needs to be bolstered in one's life. Sadly, however, many instructors stop at pointing out the student's area of weakness and fail to show how to overcome or strengthen it.

Over two centuries ago, Benjamin Franklin discussed in his autobiography the areas of weakness in his personal life. He then made the critical decision to work on those individual weaknesses and try to turn them into strengths. What a wonderful challenge for the instructor today!

We need to find areas of weakness, and then, we need to make a concentrated plan on how to overcome and strengthen the student in those particular areas. By making sure both sides of the coin are covered—the admittance of the weakness and the plan to overcome it—the student will not be discouraged nor defeated.

67

TIP #67

Insulate, but Don't Isolate

"And be not conformed to this world: but be ye transformed by the renewing of your mind, that ye may prove what is that good, and acceptable, and perfect, will of God." —Romans 12:2

"But ye are a chosen generation, a royal priesthood, an holy nation, a peculiar people; that ye should shew forth the praises of him who hath called you out of darkness into his marvellous light:"—1 Peter 2:9

The Christian instructor must understand that God's Word firmly teaches the principle of separation—that we are in the world but not of the world. In Ephesians 6:12, God's Word tells us, "*For we wrestle not against flesh and blood, but against principalities, against powers, against the rulers of the darkness of this world, against spiritual wickedness in high places.*" Because of this, we must realize we are in the position to protect those whom God has placed in our watch care.

While young people need to be taught to be salt and light, they must be careful not to become a part of the culture that surrounds them. They should never act, look, or speak like the world.

One of the best ways to accomplish this difference is to make sure the student becomes thoroughly familiar with Christ's view of the world. This Christ-centered approach will help separate the student from the norms of contemporary society.

The Lord Jesus Christ lived during the zenith of the Roman rule; yet, He was obviously, completely, and totally different from both the ruling society and the contemporary Jewish society.

We need to challenge young people to understand that they are part of a *chosen generation,* and that their actions and attitudes should testify of their sanctified and set apart lives.

68

TIP #68

Be a Memory Maker

"Wherefore I will not be negligent to put you always in remembrance of these things, though ye know them, and be established in the present truth."—2 Peter 1:12

"Hear counsel, and receive instruction, that thou mayest be wise in thy latter end."—Proverbs 19:20

Memories are created from that which is either out of the ordinary or from that which is extraordinary. People remember the unusual car they pass on the way to work. They remember the extraordinary house, be it a Hearst Castle, a Biltmore estate, or a Winchester Mystery House. They remember not the normal governmental building, but the Capitol. They do not remember the average monument, but the extraordinary one, such as the Jefferson, Lincoln, or Washington monuments.

The teacher, then, must look for ways to lift the instruction out of the meandering river of the mundane. There needs to be Niagara and Victoria-Falls moments during the course of instruction. These moments will create the memories!

True memory makers will never be forgotten. I appreciate my dad teaching us Proverbs 20:1, "*Wine is a mocker, strong drink is raging....*" I will never forget the memory of driving down Skid Row and seeing the results of alcoholism. I also appreciate my dad telling me that cigarettes would do damage to my body. It created a memory when he showed me pictures of cancer patients smoking through their esophagus. I can say that memory certainly eliminated cigarettes from ever being an attraction to me.

Perhaps a memory can be created through the use of visual aids, field trips, or a special guest speaker. Maybe the elementary instructor can make a memory by acting out a Bible story or history scene. The ideas are endless!

Inevitably, thinking of an idea and bringing it to pass takes work, yet if a memory is created, it would be a teaching moment that could last for a lifetime.

69

TIP #69

Motivate Students Toward Maximum Effort

"Whatsoever thy hand findeth to do, do it with thy might...."—Ecclesiastes 9:10

The word *motivate* could mean drive, encourage, or cajole. It could also mean goad, spur, prompt, or instigate. The instructor is the trigger for students achieving their potential. God will use you as the mentor to help them see what they can and should be doing.

We live in a world today in which mediocrity is accepted. For the Christian, however, mediocrity is a sin. God has commanded us to do things with all of our might. He has also made it clear that He approves of excellence. A study of the building of Solomon's temple and the training of the priests is a study of the excellence that God Himself mandated.

Oftentimes, instructors do not push the students, because their prodding may engender conflict and strife. The typical student does not like to be pushed! Pupils love to say, "That's good enough," or "I can't do that," when in reality, they are merely making excuses for a failure to put forth the necessary effort.

The teacher needs to challenge and motivate students to do their very best. Although it is sometimes difficult to require the extra work, writing, and reading—the end result of maximum effort will be a better equipped student.

"Continuous effort, not strength or intelligence is the key to unlocking [their] potential."—Sir Winston Churchill

70

TIP #70

Look to the Future: Forgive and Forget the Past

"The discretion of a man deferreth his anger; and it is his glory to pass over a transgression."—Proverbs 19:11

"Brethren, I count not myself to have apprehended: but this one thing I do, forgetting those things which are behind, and reaching forth unto those things which are before, I press toward the mark for the prize of the high calling of God in Christ Jesus."—Philippians 3:13–14

Every instructor can think of a time (or many times!) when he has made a mistake. I'm sure that every adult is grateful for the forgiveness he was offered for those mistakes. We also need to encourage the student to seek forgiveness. Once forgiveness has been found, he should be encouraged to go on to work for and honor the Lord.

The Apostle Paul said, "*...forgetting those things which are behind, and reaching forth unto those things which are before...*" (Philippians 3:13). Instructors, encourage the student to forget the past and to look forward to the future. (The student should also know that he has been forgiven and needs to understand that he will have a fresh start himself with the instructor.) It is vital for the teacher to encourage the student to press on, to strive for victory, and to not wallow in defeat.

Corrie ten Boom gave an excellent example of forgiveness in her book *The Hiding Place*.

> It was at a church service in Munich that I saw him, a former S.S. man who had stood guard at the shower room door in the processing center at Ravensbruck. He was the first of our actual jailers that I had seen since that time.... He came up to me as the church was emptying.... "How grateful I am for your message, Fraulein." He said. "To think that, as you say, He has washed my sins away!" His hand was thrust out to shake mine. And I, who had preached so often to the people in Bloemendaal the need to forgive, kept my hand at my side. Even as the angry, vengeful thoughts boiled through me, I saw the sin of them. Jesus Christ had died for this man; was I going to ask for more? Lord Jesus, I prayed, forgive me and help me to forgive him.... Give me Your forgiveness.
>
> As I took his hand, the most incredible thing happened. From my shoulder along my arm and through my hand a current seemed to pass from me to him, while into my heart sprang a love for this stranger that almost overwhelmed me.... When He tells us to love our enemies, He gives, along with the command, the love itself.

71

TIP #71

Communicate, Don't Negotiate

"How forcible are right words! but what doth your arguing reprove?"—Job 6:25

"Should he reason with unprofitable talk? or with speeches wherewith he can do no good?"—Job 15:3

It is astounding how so many young people in the early stages of their education, even into their junior high and high school years, have a tendency to be combative and argumentative. The instructor, however, is not there to *negotiate* with the student, but rather to *instruct* the student.

It is imperative, then, that directions are clearly stated and completely understood. This is done through communication that is exact, clear, and understandable. It is important for the instructor to discover whether or not the student understood the initial communication, as this will allow the instructor to hold the student to a certain level of responsibility.

While negotiating can be very important and helpful, when it comes to an instructor and a student, it must be clear that there is no negotiating. While compromise may be the genius of politics, it is the death knell in the classroom or the home.

It was once said, "Abraham Lincoln did not go to Gettysburg having commissioned a poll to find out what would sell in Gettysburg. There were no people with percentages for him, cautioning him about this group or that group or what they found in exit polls a year earlier. When will we have the courage of Lincoln?"

This statement should encourage the teacher to ensure that there is clear communication, that the instruction is understood, and that, consequently, the student is to be held accountable.

72

TIP #72

Develop New Skills

"The Lord will perfect that which concerneth me: thy mercy, O Lord, endureth for ever: forsake not the works of thine own hands."—Psalm 138:8

A primary responsibility of the teacher is the development of new skills in the student. The student enters the learning environment, whether the home, classroom or Sunday school room, as an unfinished project. Years ago, there was a popular little button which proclaimed, "Please be patient, God is not finished with me yet."

It is a foolish thing to think that any student is a finished product. Conversely, it is a foolish thing for us as instructors to think that we are finished products. We are also to continue growing "*in the nurture and admonition of the Lord*" (Ephesians 6:4). The training process of children or adults is one that will never be finished until either the trumpet sounds or the Lord calls us home.

We need to teach skills in areas that will make people more effective for the work of the Lord Jesus Christ. This teaching is part of developing a mind that will honour Christ. It is wise to remember how we learned some of these skills, and then seek to replicate the processes by which we were taught.

Someone once said, "Education is the most powerful weapon which you can use to change the world." Indeed, we must educate people with the Gospel of Christ. This will truly bring about change in lives. Furthermore, instructors must educate students in skills such as reading critically, thinking with discernment, solving problems, seeking solutions, and finding the answers. These skills will enable them to be used in greater ways as they strive to do the Lord's will in their lives.

73

TIP #73

Develop New Attitudes

"He that is slow to anger is better than the mighty; and he that ruleth his spirit than he that taketh a city." —Proverbs 16:32

"Hear counsel, and receive instruction, that thou mayest be wise in thy latter end."—Proverbs 19:20

The wise instructor will attempt to impact and change the student. Yet, it cannot be overemphasized that much of the learning process must be prefaced by a change in attitude. When one talks about a change in attitude, there are a variety of attitudes that can be mentioned. Attitudes that need change would include a negative attitude, a selfish attitude, a materialistic attitude, an indifferent attitude, an unforgiving attitude, and a myriad of other attitudes that would be evident to the instructor.

A quote we frequently use here at Lancaster Baptist Church is, "Attitude determines altitude." The teacher must work at developing the right attitude in the student. This mandates either a reversal, a tempering, or a re-evaluation on the part of the student. One of the most effective ways to bring this about is to ask the question, "Would Christ be pleased with my attitude?"

The instructor must learn to point out a negative attitude and then show the student how he can improve in that particular area. It is sometimes uncomfortable to point out a wrong attitude; however, it is this instruction that can bring about change in the life of the hearer.

God's Word clearly states that a wise man will hear and will increase in learning. It is so important that the student hears from the one who has a heart for him...and a heart for the things of God. It is important that he receives instruction with a right heart attitude as well.

74

TIP #74

Teach with Care and Confidence

"And ye became followers of us, and of the Lord, having received the word in much affliction, with joy of the Holy Ghost:"—1 THESSALONIANS 1:6

"And the things that thou hast heard of me among many witnesses, the same commit thou to faithful men, who shall be able to teach others also."—2 TIMOTHY 2:2

It greatly encourages the student when the instructor knows the material at hand. This helps the student understand that he can get a grasp of the subject matter. When the instructor teaches with confidence, the student can learn with confidence. (The student is further helped if he can see the steps taken to understand the material. This logistical process, in essence, is like the pathway that leads to achievement).

A teacher must teach with a God-given confidence, but he must also teach with a Christ-like care and concern. It is wise for the teacher to allow an entire group to see how a classmate has grasped the concept of truth in the material. This is especially effective with Sunday school teachers who allow students to share previous lessons that were implemented in their lives.

In years past, Wednesday nights in Baptist churches were often times of testimonies and edification of others. There were the dreaded "testifiers," who would tell a story or a blessing that had been heard scores of times before. Nevertheless, it was always a blessing when someone told how God showed him a life-changing truth. God's Word says, "*Let the redeemed of the Lord say so...*" (Psalm 107:2). This time of testimony often allowed the listeners to see the care of the Lord at work in others' lives.

The Apostle Paul said, "*Those things, which ye have...heard, and seen in me, do...*" (Philippians 4:9). Let this saying also be true for those of us who have the privilege of instructing. May we have this holy confidence, and may we always seek to communicate Christ's care and love toward others.

75

TIP #75

Be Willing to Be Vulnerable

"Hear counsel, and receive instruction, that thou mayest be wise in thy latter end."—Proverbs 19:20

Vulnerability does not come easily for those with experience in the field of education. It is difficult to admit a need for improvement, especially for strong leaders of either gender.

Part of a correct attitude toward vulnerability is to admit that we do not and cannot have all the answers ourselves. When an instructor is willing to seek counsel, correction, advice, and instruction, he is likely making a choice that will result in a more effective life. It must be remembered that, most often when counsel is given, God means it for our good. He wants us to improve in a given area.

It is never easy to admit that we do not have all the answers, and we must realize that there is always room for growth. The wise instructor will learn from parents, the pastor, the administrator, and the students. Help that is given and applied will ultimately bring more honor to God, as the teacher becomes a more effective tool for His purpose.

Therefore, it is worthwhile to open ourselves up to constructive criticism and suggestions, so that we may be more effective for our Lord.

76

TIP #76

Don't Be Afraid of the Spontaneous... Periodically

"To every thing there is a season, and a time to every purpose under the heaven:"—Ecclesiastes 3:1

V*ariety*—what a unique word! How often the humdrum of life overwhelms us and seemingly lulls us to either inaction or lack of creativity! When this uneventful routine occurs in the classroom, it would be very wise for a teacher to do something out of the ordinary—and perhaps even extraordinary! Students need variety in the classroom.

When one does something spontaneous, it is best if it is totally unexpected by the receiver. A spontaneous activity, event, or lesson will charge a class with life and will breathe a new air of excitement and refreshment into their spirits.

While it seems that the spontaneous activities are the result of the creatively fertile mind, in reality, they are nothing more than well-planned and thought-out events of the instructor! Your spontaneous activity could be a visitor who comes in to share a personal account. It could be a game, a play, a video, a class trip, or some other event that is so extraordinary the other classes will soon be talking about it!

On the other side of the coin, it must be remembered that continuity and schedule are always helpful to the teacher. If one is *always* spontaneous, he could be described as disorganized, scatterbrained, or unfocused. Because of this, it is important to understand that, while spontaneity is important, it needs to occur only periodically…lest there be too much of a good thing!

77

TIP #77

ORGANIZE, DEPUTIZE, SUPERVISE

"Take heed therefore unto yourselves, and to all the flock, over the which the Holy Ghost hath made you overseers, to feed the church of God, which he hath purchased with his own blood."—ACTS 20:28

Great teachers will learn and then teach how to effectively accomplish a task. A good English instructor, for example, teaches that a term paper is broken down into steps: bibliography cards, outline, note cards, rough draft, revision, and final copy. In teaching this order, the instructor communicates the means and methods of accomplishing a task. Whether an instructor or a pupil, one must know the proper means and methods of achieving a task.

An instructor trying to accomplish change in the life of a learner understands that effective teaching goes through these stages as well. One must first organize, then deputize, and finally, supervise.

In the education realm, organization is deciding exactly what needs to be done. This could involve deciding what books will be read and requirements will be given (requirements such as writing a book report, answering questions, or preparing for quizzes over chapters or chapter segments).

Second, deputizing involves giving the project and requirements to the student. It is imperative that the student understands exactly what is expected from him and that the expectations are reachable. It is a cause of great frustration when expectations are unrealistic. Thus, the deputizing must of necessity concentrate on clear directions, requirements, and timelines.

Finally comes the supervision. The Bible says that "*…a child left to himself bringeth his mother to shame*" (Proverbs 29:15). Likewise, it is apparent that a student left to himself often creates results that are nothing close to the intended product of the instructor.

Thus, the instructor, whether parent or teacher, must take time to organize, deputize, and supervise.

78

TIP #78

Give Students More than They Expect

"A man hath joy by the answer of his mouth: and a word spoken in due season, how good is it!"—Proverbs 15:23

It is a wonderful thing when one receives an unexpected surprise such as a personal note or phone call. Perhaps a bonus in the paycheck at an unexpected time or a small gift that comes from an unexpected source—these circumstances are unique because they are not *expected*!

It is wonderful when a student receives more than he expected to receive. It is exciting for a Sunday school class to learn more than they expected to learn.

For the schoolteacher, this element of doing the unexpected could involve bringing in a special treat made the night before. If the instructor is a man (and is challenged in the area of culinary arts), maybe a donut purchased for each person in the class could be a special treat. (Beware of Krispy Kreme glazed donuts, as the mess they make can look like a serious case of psoriasis has attacked the room!) It could be a special box of chocolates or two if the class is larger in size. (Beware of children with food allergies; be sure to accommodate their needs as well.)

For those of you who would stray from the food, maybe a handwritten note, attendance at an athletic event, a postcard, or a positive phone call to a parent could be the unexpected gesture that encourages the student in a special way.

These special moments will not soon be forgotten and could be the difference maker in allowing the student to open his heart to the truths you share.

79

TIP #79

Ask Others How You Can Improve

"Give instruction to a wise man, and he will be yet wiser: teach a just man, and he will increase in learning." —Proverbs 9:9

It is a well-known adage that unwanted advice is seldom appreciated and almost never heeded. However, God's Word says, *"A wise man will hear, and will increase learning..."* (Proverbs 1:5). It is a sign of wisdom to hear and make application. When we listen to wise counsel, it shows that we have a godly understanding.

If you desire to be a wise instructor, there are many who can help you improve. The parents of the children you teach often see things from an advantageous perspective. They will help you be more effective in your dealing with their children. A pastor will see things from an under-shepherd's perspective. He can help you have a greater spiritual impact on the lives of those who have been entrusted to you (in a Sunday school classroom as well as a school classroom). A school administrator will often help you to be more efficient and effective in the teaching process. Fellow teachers, and especially those with great experience or expertise, are more than willing to give their counsel and insight to you.

Amazingly, the only requirement to open this door of improvement, knowledge, and added efficiency is a willingness to ask. Often, that which keeps us from asking for help is pride in our skills. Greatness can be attained, and great help garnered, if we would ask those around us how we can do a better job.

80

TIP #80

Teach Biblical Decision Making

"I have chosen the way of truth: thy judgments have I laid before me."—Psalm 119:30

In recent years, the word "*values*" has come into vogue in the area of education. Much acclaim is made regarding schools that are becoming value-centered. In reality, however, values are nothing more than biblical principles. God's Word truly has the answers, and since we live in a world that is replete with questions, we must stop to consider what answers God has for today's society.

One of the most valuable lessons an instructor can teach is how to make biblically based decisions in life. The Bible provides the direction and guidance for every choice we must make in life. God's Word, according to the psalmist, is a lamp unto our feet and a light unto our paths (Psalm 119:105).

Whether for immediate decision-making or long-term planning, God's Word will guide us. When the Israelites lived in the desert climate of the Middle East, a foot lamp would often be tied to an ankle. This helped the person avoid stepping on a cold-blooded reptile that might be coiled up outside of his home. Simultaneously, a large lamp or torch was used in the same way a flashlight would be used today to light a path. The Bible has the answers for today and for our lifetime as well.

It is the instructor's responsibility, if he is truly seeking to develop the mind of Christ in his students, to show how God's Word is the final authority in all matters of faith and practice. A wise instructor will teach his students to ask, "What would Jesus do?" or "What does the Bible teach?" Such questions will help them in their life decisions.

Value-centered education is, in reality for the Christian, nothing more than biblical precepts put into practice. May you influence the next generation to make Christ-honoring and Bible-based decisions!

81

TIP #81

FREQUENTLY LAUGH WITH, NEVER LAUGH AT

"For God giveth to a man that is good in his sight wisdom, and knowledge, and joy:"—ECCLESIASTES 2:26

The book of Proverbs says, "*A merry heart doeth good like a medicine: but a broken spirit drieth the bones*" (Proverbs 17:22). There is no doubt in my mind that the Lord Jesus Christ had a joy and a merriment about Him. This conclusion is based on the fact that the little children wanted to come to Him. Have you ever seen a person in church or school who has a broken or hardened spirit? Usually, this person has a limited ministry in training young people.

One of the greatest attributes an instructor can have is that of a positive and joyful spirit. There is no question that a happy and fun-loving demeanor is advantageous in creating a positive learning relationship. This spirit, which is often called camaraderie, creates a unity and a bond that helps progress to be attained.

On the other side, a great mistake can be made when laughter is directed at, rather than with, the student. One of the most unkind things an instructor can do is laugh at a student's mistake or ill-timed question. The Word of God states that "*...the Lord...hath not left off his kindness to the living and to the dead...*"(Ruth 2:20). When students feel that one of their own is an underdog or is being made fun of, the instructor is often shut out and hence, the learning process is hindered.

The place of instruction should be a place of joy. This joy should be one of companionship, friendship, achievement, camaraderie, and most of all, it should be a joy of the Lord.

82

TIP #82

Inspire Yourself Before Seeking to Inspire Others

"But there is a spirit in man: and the inspiration of the Almighty giveth them understanding."—Job 32:8

It is usually true that the student will never be more excited about the subject matter than the instructor is. This statement mandates that the instructor be inspired before attempting to transfer truth.

There are a number of ways that an effective instructor can seek inspiration before entering the educational arena. The most permanent source of inspiration is the Word of God. When one realizes the life-changing potential of God's Word when applied to a willing heart, the teacher and student alike will be inspired. The Word of God must be fresh and inspiring to us before we can be fresh and inspiring to those who are entrusted to our care.

After the great primacy source of the Word of God, there are other resources that can help the instructor to be effective in inspiring his students. These tools include reading books that deal with the subject matter, writing encouraging notes, and maintaining a "blessing book" in which you can record blessings from the Lord. Sometimes, inspiration is found through great poetry, quotations, or even a challenging and motivating tape or CD.

This "priming of the emotional and mental pump" enables the instructor to pull from his knowledge a stream of water that will be refreshing and inspiring to the recipients.

83

TIP #83

Teach Them to Lead by Making Them Read

"The heart of the prudent getteth knowledge; and the ear of the wise seeketh knowledge."—Proverbs 18:15

It has often been quoted that "readers are leaders." Many decades ago Charles Jones said, "You will be the same person five years from now as you are today, except for the books you read and the people you are around." If this is true, and I have no doubt as to its veracity, it is incumbent on both the parent and teacher to provoke the learner toward reading.

One of the best ways to help young people with reading is to make sure that good material is available to them. In the early stages of reading, it is often true that a "taste" must be developed. Therefore, the instructor must find material that entertains, as well as educates.

Frequently, the material that would scintillate the mature reader is far too difficult for those at the early stages of reading and comprehension. The instructor is responsible to find material, whether books or magazines, that is at the proper educational level for the readers.

In order to develop this habit of reading, reading must be required and encouraged. Books and magazines need to be made available. Articles need to be copied and handed out. It is extremely profitable to have a library available in both the church and the school. It is undoubtedly incumbent upon the parent who is serious about furthering the child's education to make books readily accessible in the home.

While reading is a wonderful tool and a necessary ingredient for growth, there is also poison which must be averted. The wise parent and instructor will guard the students and will do their best to steer them away from authors and philosophies that could ultimately bring ruin.

84

TIP #84

Pass the Credit, and Accept the Blame

"For whosoever exalteth himself shall be abased; and he that humbleth himself shall be exalted."—Luke 14:11

God's Word states in Isaiah 42:8 that God will not give His glory to another. As instructors, we must teach students to give God glory. James 1:17 clearly delineates that all good things come from God. In a world full of pride, we must constantly be on guard to give God the credit, for we owe Him everything.

Not only must we give God glory for victories He has given, we must be willing to accept blame for mistakes we have committed and problems we have caused. Americans today have developed a "blame-shifting" mentality that frequently refuses to be held accountable for anything. Everything is someone else's fault. This mentality runs contrary to the biblical precept clearly shown in the life of Peter. Upon hearing the cock crow he "*...wept bitterly*" (Luke 22:62), and then repented for his wrongdoing.

Willingness to bear the blame, to admit a wrongdoing, and to accept the penalty is an obvious sign of maturation. When taken in the lives of students, these steps need to receive the highest commendation and praise. This humble attitude is an important step toward rightful prioritization in one's thinking. When a person's thinking is corrected, it will inevitably result in changes of behavior and in life in general.

A great threat to this philosophy is the fact that we feel a tremendous need to allow others to know what we have accomplished. However, the Bible states, "*Let another man praise thee, and not thine own mouth*" (Proverbs 27:2). If we can humbly deflect the glory to God when praise is offered, we will truly be doing that which is pleasing in his sight.

85

TIP #85

Create an Atmosphere Conducive to Learning

"For God is not the author of confusion, but of peace, as in all churches of the saints."—1 Corinthians 14:33

When the space shuttle is being prepared for liftoff, much conversation is dedicated to the subject of atmospheric conditions. Those who are knowledgeable in the area of flying (whether it is here, close to *terra firma*, or in outer space) know that atmospheric conditions can make a voyage either extremely unpleasant or very enjoyable. In a similar way, the instructor must understand that conditions under his control will have an effect on the learning process as a whole.

Part of creating an environment conducive to learning involves eliminating objects that might lessen the impact of truth. Hindrances could include the placement of chairs, the teaching background, or other distractions.

Many other conditions that can be controlled by the teacher, in areas such as cleanliness and orderliness, will have a substantial impact on the educational process. In 1 Corinthians 14:40, God's Word states, *"Let all things be done decently and in order."* While it is true that "cleanliness is next to godliness" is not a biblical principle, it is a practical principle.

A leader in the area of instruction will peruse the learning environment to remedy or improve a pre-existing condition. Words such as, *professional, pristine, excellent, neat,* and *orderly,* are all descriptions that should be jealously sought after by the instructor.

86

TIP #86

Let the Students Know You Have Big Dreams for Them

"Where there is no vision, the people perish: but he that keepeth the law, happy is he."—Proverbs 29:28

God's Word states in Joel 2:28, "...*your old men shall dream dreams, your young men shall see visions.*" The most important thing an instructor can do is create a vision in the hearts and minds of the students. It is not always possible to emulate Martin Luther's teacher, who bowed before his class and said he knew not what greatness sat before him. However, it is essential for the instructor to encourage the student to go beyond the stricture of mediocrity ... to strive to do something of significance for the King of kings.

The instructor wears many hats and has many roles. The chief of these roles is that of visionary, dream caster, or even as one business calls it, "chief imaginaire." The teacher must dream big for his students! Oftentimes, it simply takes belief and understanding in the student to know that he can and will accomplish something of eternal significance. Once this fact is accepted, it becomes easier to act upon those dreams with a change in both act and behavior.

The student must dream about the results of gaining knowledge! The student must be taught that the Bible can be learned, and more importantly, lived. The student must learn through the educational venue that growth, although painful, is necessary and advantageous. The student in the Sunday school class needs to see that spiritual growth can be accomplished.

Unfortunately, many times the instructor's dreams are never verbalized. Because of this, a seed of potential is never germinated. Let those you mentor know that you have big dreams for them! It is of great worth to the student to know there is someone who believes he can and will succeed.

87

TIP #87

Instruct Outside of the Classroom

"Pleasant words are as an honeycomb, sweet to the soul, and health to the bones."—Proverbs 16:24

True education goes beyond the boundaries of a fifty-minute class hour. One of the methods in which the instructor can create a kinship with his students is through contact at insular events. At these times, an encouraging word can be spoken, applications can be made, and even corrective statements can be directed to the student.

For the schoolteacher, this type of contact could mean attending games, plays, or recitals. Increased effectiveness will also occur when a note is sent to comment on the child's involvement in one of these events. When the venue is outside of the normal operating arena, this "second-mile" effort is greatly appreciated.

For the Sunday school teacher, this special touch could be a kind comment at a visitation dinner, a church event, or once again, an encouraging note. The Sunday school teacher can also encourage a student who participated in a cantata or special music number. This heartfelt appreciation will make the student prone to accept directives from that particular authority figure.

For the parent, it can be stated that *no* event is outside the realm in which attendance would be appropriate. This type of special instruction might involve doing the unexpected or performing random acts of kindness that go beyond the "norm."

May each of us as mentors provide encouragement and loving direction when *outside* of the regular teaching arena! May our heartfelt words and kind actions be sweet to the soul and health to the bones of those whom we seek to influence!

88

TIP #88

Always Provide for Needs, and Sometimes Supply the Wants

"But my God shall supply all your need according to his riches in glory by Christ Jesus."—Philippians 4:19

Any mentor should know and communicate what general requirements are expected in his particular area of influence, whether it is the home, classroom, basketball court, or ball field. These core requirements, whether obeying immediately, respecting authority, honoring God, or soulwinning are not easily transferred to the student in today's society. It is then imperative that, despite the difficulty of the principle transference, the instructor perseveres to teaching core truths, values, and precepts that will help the student live a Christ-pleasing life.

One must understand that the flesh rebels against the discipline of both learning and change. However, this does not constitute a valid reason for laying aside the responsibility of training the next generation! The educational journey is an uphill climb. It entails an arduous effort on behalf of the instructor who is serious about ensuring the transference of truth. Education is a need for students, and it must be provided by the committed teacher!

The core necessities of teaching must represent an educational skeleton around which everything else remains in the peripheral position. However, it is also valid to occasionally surprise students with events, such as field trips, that allow for a break from the routine learning process.

These "mini-vacations" from the usual learning process are best served if they are both brief and unexpected. When Jesus told Peter to go out into the deep, this undoubtedly surprised him, yet his obedience was rewarded in a most memorable way! It is also gratifying for the student to see something which he has looked forward to (such as a planned educational event) come to pass.

As teachers, let us strive to always meet the educational needs of our students. But remember—it's okay to supply the educational "wants," as well!

89

TIP #89

Say What You Mean, and Mean What You Say

"Providing for honest things, not only in the sight of the Lord, but also in the sight of men."—2 Corinthians 8:21

"But above all things, my brethren, swear not, neither by heaven, neither by the earth, neither by any other oath: but let your yea be yea; and your nay, nay; lest ye fall into condemnation."—James 5:12

God's Word says, "*...let your yea be yea; and your nay, nay...*" (James 5:12). Down through the early decades of American history, it was said that a man's word should be his bond. Today, more than ever before, the teacher's words must be a source of truth and absolute validity. The godly mentor, in the classroom, Sunday school room, or home, must take great care to not impeach himself by creating questions or doubt in the mind of the student.

Proper research, and exactness in the telling and teaching are of extraordinary importance. If the student cannot trust the teacher, the instructional process is severely crippled. I thank the Lord that since the instructors of my children have always been in a Christian venue, their teaching has been inextricably tied to both the Word of God and the place of our worship. These instructors have been truthful and clear in their teaching, and hence, my children have been able to trust and learn from them.

A teacher must learn that equivocation or circular reasoning will often confuse the student and soon make it more difficult to communicate truth. Any deviation from the truth affects every area of the students' lives, and the instructor's authority will be brought into question.

Jesus Christ is our great example of one who said what He meant and meant what He said. This truth is captured in a description of Jesus found in the Gospel of Matthew when "*He spake as one having authority*" (Matthew 7:2).

May our words as teachers be acceptable in the sight of the Lord, and may we seek to be concise and truthful in our instruction to the next generation!

90

TIP #90

Look to the Future, but Value and Enjoy Today

"It is of the Lord's mercies that we are not consumed, because his compassions fail not. They are new every morning: great is thy faithfulness."—Lamentations 3:22–23

Several years ago, David Ogilvy wrote in his autobiography that if there was a singular thing he could change in his life, it would be that he would have taken time to "smell the roses" and enjoy the victories he had won instead of always pressing on for bigger and better things. The importance of goals cannot be denied or neglected, yet we must take time to teach the student how much we have to thank the Lord for on a daily basis.

The Bible teaches us that Heaven is truly a wonderful place, surpassing even our most grandiose human expectations. It is a place for which we are to live and anticipate. However, the Scriptures also say, "*This is the day which the Lord hath made; we will rejoice and be glad in it*" (Psalm 118:24). The instructor must teach the student that each day is truly a gift from God and that the senses we enjoy, the freedoms we share, and the possibilities we have are gifts from our Creator.

It is good to plan and think ahead, but it is also beneficial to stop, to think, and to thank. Take time and see that the Lord is good. His faithfulness is great, and His blessings are without number. Let's not take for granted blessings we enjoy on a daily basis because of the goodness of our God. It is still true that thinkfulness will lead to thankfulness.

91

TIP #91

Have More Teaching Material than You Think You Will Need

"Prepare thy work without, and make it fit for thyself in the field; and afterwards build thine house."—Proverbs 24:27

When the instructor enters the educational arena, it is always best to have a surplus of material. This concept of teaching out of the overflow with no threat of the well running dry accomplishes several things. It allows the instructor to feel more at ease and removes any concern of running out of resource material. This will help the student feel as if the instructor is well-versed and excited about the subject at hand.

This fresh influx of material, while adding to the previously researched body of work, creates an atmosphere of immediacy and urgency. This is contrasted by yellowing pages that merely contain the "dry bones" of a thought (that now has long since lost its relevance and importance). While it is true that there is nothing new under the sun, there does need to be an attempt on the part of the instructor to continue to add to the body of a certain subject. By adding to the collected material, the instructor will be forced to constantly whittle out that which is possibly outdated and less relevant, in favor of that which is fresh and applicable.

Experienced instructors will agree that it is much easier to reduce the time given to a certain subject because of the surplus of material, than it is to try to stretch out those last ten minutes with three minutes of material that is at hand.

92

TIP #92

Identify and Improve

"For I know that in me (that is, in my flesh,) dwelleth no good thing: for to will is present with me; but how to perform that which is good I find not."—Romans 7:18

One of the most important goals an instructor can accomplish is to help the student see where there is need for improvement. Because it is difficult to admit personal weakness, confessing a need for improvement is often equally as difficult. Although the Scripture clearly states that in ourselves there *"dwelleth no good thing,"* we find this verse easier to apply to others than to ourselves.

Learning and improvement usually begin with the admittance of need or weakness in a particular area. The instructor must help the student understand that attaining a certain skill level is not acceptable—doing your best is acceptable. The old adage, "Good, better, best—never let it rest until your good is better and your better is best," needs to be dusted off and used to challenge a new generation of students.

The teacher cannot stop with simply pointing out or even dissecting a weakness, because this could lead to a malaise of indifference. The instructor's primary job is not the finding of the fault, but teaching the student how the fault can be conquered and ultimately overcome.

Victory is achievable and, with God's help, great change can transpire. One of the first steps toward victory is to encourage the student in every way possible to overcome his weakness. Once the student begins to see growth and accompanying change, this could be a motivation in and of itself.

93

TIP #93

Offer Your Best

"Whatsoever thy hand findeth to do, do it with thy might…."
—Ecclesiastes 9:10

The constant challenge facing teachers is determining how much to invest in the instructional effort. While we have heard that it is a sin to do less than our best, we all realize that there are restraints in both time and energy that sometimes limit us in doing what we could or should.

The challenge of doing your best is one that, when heeded, always brings fruition.

When the instructor truly has the students' best interests in his heart, he will ask himself this question, "How can I do a better job, and how can I best bring about the transference of truth?" As the Holy Spirit gives us direction or when suggestions are offered by those who are trying to help us be more effective, it is up to us to avail ourselves of every opportunity to do the best possible job. In doing this, we will see fruit in the lives of those we mentor.

It is important to realize the extreme brevity of time in which true instruction is actually possible, whether it is the school year, the Sunday school year, or even the years parents have their children at home. God's Word states that we are to "*take therefore no thought for the morrow....*" With that in mind, we need to capture the day that God has given us. We must seize every opportunity in which we have a chance to impact the lives that have been entrusted to us.

94

TIP #94

Model Integrity

"In all things shewing thyself a pattern of good works: in doctrine shewing uncorruptness, gravity, sincerity," —Titus 2:7

"That ye may approve things that are excellent; that ye may be sincere and without offence till the day of Christ;" —Philippians 1:10

After laboriously working to produce a vase or a jar, artists in ancient Rome often faced a dilemma. They would sometimes detect a crack after removing the pottery from the kiln. This forced them to make a choice to either destroy the object and start over, or to attempt to camouflage the weakness and pass the vessel off as one without defect. The weakness was camouflaged by filling the crack with wax and painting over the vessel. To the untrained eye, it was difficult to detect the weakness that existed in the vessel. This led craftsmen who had vessels without flaws to put above their pottery the Latin phrase, *sine cera*. This is where we get our word *sincere*, meaning "without wax."

Interestingly enough, the way to detect wax in a vessel was to hold it up against a bright light. Today, we as teachers, whether in the home or classroom, need to constantly hold our lives up to our light, the Lord Jesus Christ.

It is crucial for the instructor to be sincere—to "walk the talk." It is important for the mentor to live a life of transparency and integrity.

Shakespeare, in his play *Hamlet*, had his character Polonius say, "This above all, to thine own self be true." The Christian today ought to say, "This above all, to the Lord Jesus Christ be true."

95

TIP #95

Focus on the Root, Not Just the Fruit

"A good man out of the good treasure of the heart bringeth forth good things: and an evil man out of the evil treasure bringeth forth evil things."—MATTHEW 12:35

Some parents and teachers are quick to see a problem and then try to attack it. The experienced instructor will understand that a fruit problem is always connected to a root problem. What is the core problem that is bringing forth bad fruit? Maybe a child in school or Sunday school is wearing clothes that are not Christ-honoring. The question must be asked, "Why do they want to wear this particular type of clothing?"

In Proverbs 4:23, God's Word says, *"Keep thy heart with all diligence; for out of it are the issues of life."* Therefore, it is wise for the instructor to teach and affect the heart. As the heart is shaped, so goes the life.

One of the great flaws of contemporary fundamentalism is the judgment solely based on the exterior. One might say, "This person has a good haircut, is dressed in a neat manner, and is obeying the rules; therefore, he must be an extremely fine person." In reality, he could be talking about a group of men who are incarcerated and who have no choice as to their haircut, who have to follow rules regarding their uniform, and who have to obey the warden or suffer severe consequences. The outward conformity may be present, but the heart may be far from what God would have it to be.

May we see beyond the fruit problem and beyond the outward conformity, and may we look to the root problem in the lives of our students! May we patiently teach them that as they delight in the Lord (as opposed to delighting in the ungodliness of the day) they will see the results of proper fruit in due season (Psalm 1)!

96

TIP #96

NEVER GIVE UP

"I have fought a good fight, I have finished my course, I have kept the faith:"—2 TIMOTHY 4:7

The Sunday school teacher, pastor, and schoolteacher have all experienced the desire to see their students growing in the Lord. Yet, every mentor understands the frustration that occurs when a lesson is repeated multitudinous times without producing the desired effect. When this feeling of frustration occurs, one must never give up! The instructor never knows how close he is to seeing fruit in the life of the student.

When the stonecutter cleanly divides the piece of granite, it was not the hundredth blow that broke the rock; it was a compilation of all one hundred blows. This repetitive action eventually allows the small fissure to become a place of cleaving.

It is easy for the instructor to say, "No one is listening," "They will not change," or "This lesson makes no difference." But, the instructor must understand and realize that repetition is truly a great aid in learning! (While it is necessary to repeat truths and principles until the student assimilates them, it is also necessary to make sure there is understanding and application.)

Satan will do everything in his power to stop the instructor from attempting to touch the lives of others. It is at this time that we are reminded to be faithful and to continue to stand in the gap for the next generation. Let us seek the Lord's help as we stay committed to His cause!

97

TIP #97

Teach Respect

"Be kindly affectioned one to another with brotherly love; in honour preferring one another;"—ROMANS 12:10

God's Word says to give honor to whom honor is due (Romans 13:7). Not only should we honor people, we should also give honor to worthy institutions and principles. God has given three institutions: the home, the church, and the government. When proper respect is given to these institutions, behavioral conformity will follow the dictates of the Word of God.

During the nineteenth century, American schools and churches put great effort into teaching respect for God, family, and country. Teaching respect is still needed today, as it was over one hundred years ago.

The instructor must understand that this respect is not natural and runs contrary to our carnal nature. He must teach his pupils both how to respect and what to respect. (God's Word teaches us to obey our parents and to pray for those in authority over us. Obedience and prayer are good actions to incorporate when teaching respect.) The student must understand that respect for God, the church, and family is something that is pleasing to God.

"Some people may respect you some or even all of the time. However, I believe the greatest compliment a teacher can have is the true respect of his students."—A future teacher

98

TIP #98

Hold the Student to a High Standard

"That ye may approve things that are excellent; that ye may be sincere and without offence till the day of Christ;"
—Philippians 1:10

Growing up in a home where a "C" on a test or report card was anathema has led me to encourage my children toward academic excellence. The world in which we live seems content to accept the average, the norm, or the mediocre.

It is incumbent upon the instructor to challenge the student to improve. Bob Moawod said, "Average is the place in the middle. It is the best of the worst or the worst of the best." The great English leader, Oliver Cromwell, said, "Those who stop being better stop being good." The great composer Toscanini said, "No one knows the best he can do." Yet, oftentimes, teachers settle for "average" in the lives of their pupils instead of pressing for excellence and improvement.

Requiring a high standard will necessitate additional work on the part of both the instructor and the student. Whether in the grading or the preparation, a price will be paid for going beyond the accepted norms.

After all, it is high standards and excellent workmanship in which people are interested after the passage of time. For example, the vocal virtuosity of Caruso or the magnificent artistic skills of Leonardo da Vinci or Michelangelo, are still receiving the plaudits of the world. At some point in time, the reformer must realize that there are unique and enormous benefits to paying a higher price. May we be the mentors to guide them to that realization.

99

TIP #99

Challenge the Student to Sacrifice Good...for Great

"I beseech you therefore, brethren, by the mercies of God, that ye present your bodies a living sacrifice, holy, acceptable unto God, which is your reasonable service."—Romans 12:1

Our lives are a compilation of choices we make. All too often, our choices involve settling for something that is good, instead of doing that which is great.

The instructor must teach the student that all choices have long-term results. Joshua 24:15 says, *"Choose you this day whom ye will serve,"* but there are a multitude of other choices besides choosing to serve the Lord. Are we willing to be wholehearted Christians? Are we willing to walk a holy life? Are we willing to be described as an Acts 20:20 and Matthew 28:19-20 Christian? If this is so, the choice will be made to sacrifice what could be good for things of far greater importance and far better long-term results.

It is good to catch a few extra minutes of sleep, but it is great to get up and have devotions in the morning. It is good to enjoy a delicious meal, but it is great to take care of our bodies so we strengthen them...and potentially lengthen our ministry. It is good to have an enjoyable time doing things we want to do, but it is great to give our lives in ministry to others.

The instructor should help the student realize that the sacrifices made during our short tenure on earth will reap dividends that will last for eternity. The student needs to approach the choices regarding the expenditure of life and ask, "Will this use of my time—and my life—be for something that is good or for something that is truly great?"

100

TIP #100

Don't Give or Take Excuses

"The soul that sinneth, it shall die. The son shall not bear the iniquity of the father, neither shall the father bear the iniquity of the son: the righteousness of the righteous shall be upon him, and the wickedness of the wicked shall be upon him."—Ezekiel 18:20

It has been said that an excuse is nothing more than a lie wrapped in the skin of a reason. From the instructor's standpoint, there are 101 excuses why we do not have time to go the extra mile. Some of the favorites include: "We are too tired," "We are too busy," "We are too stressed," "We are too overworked," "We have too many things on our plates." In reality, we need to understand that these are nothing more than just excuses.

One of the critical components in this is that we will have time to do what is important to us. Rather than making excuses, we need to realize that a leader will find a way. Conversely, students have been in the process of making excuses for generations upon generations. Although we laugh at the humorous excuses about why homework was not done (which includes some of the most creative storytelling in the annuls of modern man), in reality, we realize we need to hold people accountable.

It is critical for instructors to disallow excuses. This teaches the aspect of accountability.

The Bible says that some day we will give an account at the Judgment Seat of Christ. The student who learns that we are accountable for the things we do or do not do, will be making a tremendous step in the right direction.

101

TIP #101

Live with Eternity in View

"And now, little children, abide in him; that, when he shall appear, we may have confidence, and not be ashamed before him at his coming."—1 John 2:28

The return of Christ is the purpose of our instruction and the reason for our investment in the lives of others. There is a Heaven, and there is a Hell. There is a Judgment Seat, and there is a Great White Throne Judgment. There is a time when crowns will be distributed so that we may give those crowns back to our Lord and Saviour.

There will come a day when the car we drove, the house we lived in, the deer we shot, the fish we caught, and the sports we followed will seem so insignificant that we will wonder why we did not do more for the Saviour.

John Bunyan, in his great work, *Pilgrim's Progress*, helped us understand that Christian, the one who pictured the believer, did his best when his eyes were fixed on the Celestial City. Like Christian, we also need to leave our burden at the foot of the Cross. We need to dissuade ourselves from the distractions and the paths that lead us away from what our Saviour would have us to do. We need to truly look to Jesus, concentrate on the decisions that will last forever, and live with eternity in view.

Also available from
Striving Together Publications

Abiding in Christ

Dr. Paul Chappell

This unique study of John 15 takes you on a journey of learning how to become more like Christ by abiding in Him on a daily basis. (160 Pages, Paperback)

It's a Wonderful Life

Terrie Chappell

In these pages, Terrie Chappell shares a practical, biblical approach to loving your family and serving Jesus Christ. Her humorous and down-to-earth insight will encourage your heart and equip you to love the life to which God has called you. (280 Pages, Hardback)

Ten Principles for Biblical Living

Dr. Don Sisk

In these pages, Dr. Don Sisk, veteran missionary and former president of Baptist International Missions Inc., shares the ten biblical principles that have shaped his life, his marriage, and his ministry through nearly six decades of faithfulness to Christ. (120 Pages, Hardback)

strivingtogether.com

Adult/Teen

Sunday **School** Curriculum

Abiding in Christ

This unique study of John 15 takes you on a journey of learning how to become more like Christ by abiding in Him on a daily basis. The teacher's guide and student guide makes a perfect curriculum for adult classes in your church.

Discover Your Destiny

Discover what every young adult needs to know about making right choices in a world full of wrong. This seventeen lesson series will equip students to discover the perfect will of God for their lives. The teacher's guide contains lesson outlines, teaching ideas, and Scripture helps.

Hook, Line & Sinker

Twenty-one weeks of powerful lessons for both teens and parents! This material can be used for adults, for teens, or for both at the same time! It will greatly strengthen the families of your church by unmasking the lies of the enemy.

strivingtogether.com

strivingtogether
done.